WHY ME
LORD?!

Suffering Widower

DALLAS M. GARDNER

ISBN 979-8-88751-381-2 (paperback)
ISBN 979-8-88751-382-9 (digital)

Christian Faith Publishing
832 Park Avenue
Meadville, PA 16335
www.christianfaithpublishing.com

Printed in the United States of America

To my wife, Marla, and our sons—Jordan, Andrew, Jacob, and Dallas Aron—who were and still are the absolute apple of their mother's eye!

To Marla's closest friend; her sister, Misty Jane; and her mother, Mary. And to another beautiful lady, Christina, who brought love and the enjoyment of life back.

CONTENTS

INTRODUCTION

The title of the book has a very significant and very dear meaning to me. When I was a small child, I would stand in front of the Zenith console phonograph stereo my parents owned, and I would sing along with the small 45 record of Kris Kristofferson's "Why Me, Lord?"[1]. If you don't remember or have never heard of the song, here are the lyrics from http://www.songlyrics.com/kris-kristofferson/why-me-lord-lyrics/.

Verse 1:
Why me, Lord?
What have I ever done,
To deserve even one,
Of the pleasure I've known,
Tell me, Lord,
What did I ever do,
That was worth lovin' You,
For the kindness You've shown,

Chorus:
Lord, help me, Jesus,
I've wasted it, so help me, Jesus,
I know what I am,
But now that I know,
That I needed you, so help me, Jesus,
My soul's in your hand,

---

[1]   Kris Kristofferson, "Why Me," (2022), https://www.songlyrics.com.

Verse 2:
Try me, Lord,
If you think there's a way,
I can try to repay,
All I've takin' from you,
Maybe, Lord,
I can show someone else,
What I've been through myself,
On my way back to you.

The lyrics to this song have taken on a whole different meaning for me, especially the second verse. A dual meaning of both intense pain but also one of unbelievable honor. The excruciating pain of why the events you will read about took place. But ultimately what I then understood to be the enormous honor of being selected to endure a very miniscule fraction of the suffering Jesus endured. Just as the apostles rejoiced in the book Acts 5:41 that they had been worthy to be dishonored on behalf of the name—the name of Jesus.

After many months of searching desperately for answers to why, begging for some release from the suffering, I heard a still-small voice tell me that I was not the only one who suffered far greater calamities. God also reminded me that for many years, I had prayed to be more like Jesus. Jesus, do You think there's a way I could try to repay the gifts You gave? That maybe I could show someone else what I've been through myself. To bring someone closer, or to find their way to you.

I have never once considered myself a writer, nor growing up did I ever envision that I would one day attempt to write anything other than something that was assigned to me in some class. But regardless of how someone views themselves or plans their path in life, God allows an event to take place that completely diverts the trajectory you thought you were on.

Why then has someone who thought they would never write a book attempt to do so, you may ask? Well, here is what happened to lead me to this undertaking. In January of 2017, I lost my father to an infection similar to a Methicillin-resistant Staphylococcus aureus (MRSA) infection. He was eighty-one (less than seventeen days from his eighty-second birthday) and, up until a year before this date, had really never been in a hospital.

In July of 2017, my beautiful wife woke up with excruciating pain in her abdomen. We believed, at the time, it was appendicitis. In September of 2018, she died of colon cancer.

In late 2018, my mother who had heart surgery in 2016 was told her condition had regressed back to what it was before the surgery. In October of 2019, she died of heart failure. One might say that I have had my fair share of grief.

First of all, let me say that I am a disciple of Jesus Christ. I say it this way because I believe that simply to say that one is a Christian in today's climate has lost the meaning that it once held or has become nothing more than a mere label that some people place upon themselves but really denotes that they merely have a belief in God. I believe, in today's society, this term does not have the true meaning it once held. Just as C. S. Lewis describes in his book *Mere Christianity*.

Another title that I hold is that of widower. This is a title that I do not wish upon my worst enemy. But unfortunately, I see the glaring contrast in how the death of a spouse is endured between women and men. A woman may grieve for many years and also may decide to never enter a relationship again. Whereas the majority of men have been taught that a "real" man does not show any emotion, good or bad, right or wrong. So many, if not most, men tend not to express their profound love for their spouse. Couple that with the universal standard that perceived real men absolutely do not expose their wounds, especially mental or emotional wounds in any way whatsoever.

Additionally, men are wired to go into this automatic repair response. I need to fix what it is that is broken. So for most men, you have this scenario unfold. I am a man. I am not supposed to show my wound. I need to fix what is broken. The thing that is broken is that I don't have a spouse anymore. I need to find a new spouse as soon as I can; problem solved.

For me, it was not the case, and I believe for many men, if they are honest, that is not the case either. If they would simply allow themselves just a moment to not rush to try and fix things.

Once the dust settled after the memorial and funeral events after the death of my wife, I began to search for some resources that might help process what I had just experienced. I realized very quickly that there is a vast number of books dedicated to dealing with grief, and there are many which are specifically aimed at widows; but there is significantly less information available for men who are grieving the loss of their wives. There are numerous reasons as to why this disparity exists. These explanations range from how men grieve to how men view this type of wound, as I stated above. As well as the fact that there are statistically approximately three times as many widows as widowers.

After a couple of years of struggling with what I felt was an urging from God to share what He taught me during this time, with the hope that I might help someone who is or has been through the same thing, I had felt completely lacking of any ability to do this sort of thing. But regardless, I know one thing is certain: when you feel compelled by God to do something, it will accomplish what He wants it to accomplish regardless of what you think might happen. Just as He said in Isaiah 55:11, speaking about Scripture, "so My word that comes from My mouth will not return to Me empty, but it will accomplish what I please and will prosper in what I send it to do."[2]

No matter how big or how small the results may appear, in the human sense, it will bring forth the results that God desires it to bring. And if that is just one person who is impacted, then that will be worth it.

This book is not written with the viewpoint of being a self-help guide; rather, it is meant to provide an example of how *the* living God spoke through and revealed Himself to a man who was at the lowest possible point of his life. A Christian man who began to question why these events were allowed to happen and why weren't his prayers answered in the way he wanted. This is to testify the journey I want to take you on and, as I said earlier, allow God to use this book in any way he sees fit.

---

[2] All biblical references are taken from Holman Christian Standard Bible (Nashville, Tennessee: Holman Bible Publishers, 2012).

CHAPTER 1

Flashback, Not a Typical Start

It was during the summer of 1991, after I had transferred from one college to another, that I ended up on a trip to Myrtle Beach, South Carolina, with some friends from high school. Little did I know that I would meet my future wife, Marla Elizabeth Shelton, on this trip. Neither one of us had a clue as to what God had in store during this trip. Marla was completely unaware that there could be anything of the sort about to transpire because at the time, she was dating another boy who was not on the trip but was back in Tennessee. I, however, was single and looking to find a girl to start dating. I wasn't necessarily looking for this during this beach trip, but I was quite open to the idea. I had no clue that I would travel hundreds of miles away to meet a girl who lived in the same town that I did.

We met by happenstance, as the friends that I was there with were mutual friends with the group of Marla and her friends, many of whom, including Marla, worked together at the Little Caesars Pizza restaurant in our hometown of Greeneville, Tennessee. This happened to be Marla's high school graduation beach trip. As you might be guessing, there were some less-than-Christian activities that were taking place during this trip. As a matter of fact, one reason that I was invited to this trip was because I had just turned twenty-one years old the previous January, and I was capable of supplying the group with alcoholic beverages.

Keep in mind this was long before everyone had a cell phone. But somehow, which is unknown to me to this day, all these individuals got together one night to socialize and have a good time in the condominium that we were staying in. Some of the group had already been having a good time and were not quite feeling well. Some of the group, including myself, had been coming to this beach for many years, and the allure of the nightlife just didn't have the appeal that it once had when we were younger; so we were simply having a good time in the condo.

It was at this point that Marla began having somewhat of an attack of anxiety, which I believe was most likely caused by her pining for this boyfriend back home. I don't remember ever discussing the cause of the anxiety that she was feeling that night, but I am sure that it came up somewhere during our marriage.

I became aware that Marla was not feeling well that night, and I asked her if she would like to go for a walk and get away from the room and the people for a bit. I actually had no ulterior motive behind this action because I had not, up to this point, looked at Marla through the lens of attraction. The amusing thing about the whole situation was that I had been attempting to woo some of her other friends that night. But by God's grace, she actually took me up on the walk.

We left the room and went down to the street and walked down around to the neighboring hotel. This hotel had a hot tub that was next to the outdoor pool. I remember asking her if she would like to relax in the hot tub for a bit, but I don't think that we did. We then ended up walking down the beach under the moonlight and getting to know each other. I do remember trying to hold her hand as we walked, but she would not. With that gesture, I did not attempt anything else because I would never force myself on someone who was not interested. We ended up back at the room after what was actually a quite brief excursion, and that was the last that I talked with Marla on this trip. We all returned to our hometown of Greeneville, Tennessee, and got back to the things we were doing before the trip. Marla was completely unaware during the trip, but she was actually pregnant by the boyfriend.

Two years went by, and I didn't do very well with my academic and college football careers. I had been academically suspended from one university due to not passing enough hours, which caused me to miss the last season that I could play football due to NCAA eligibility rules. I really didn't want to delay graduating college any longer; at this point, I just wanted to be done. For me, college was just a way to keep playing football, and I had very little interest in actually finishing with a degree. But I did manage to pass the necessary credit hours within the core academic areas, so I was close to being able to graduate with a degree. I just needed to pick a concentration and finish.

Due to the academic suspension, I transferred again and basically was floating academically for a brief period of time. After an economics course in which I did very well, I changed my major to business. I was able to finish and graduate with a bachelor's degree in May of 1993. Then the process of finding a job began.

At some point in the years, between the years of 1991 to 1993, I had been dating a younger girl that attended the same high school. She was a freshman when I was a senior, but we didn't get together until, I believe, her senior year. We dated for a few years, and during her first year of college—sometime in the fall of 1992, I believe—she broke it off. I really never knew the reason behind her decision to end the relationship, but it hurt nonetheless.

In June of 1993, Marla had found out that I was not dating anyone. Again, this is way before cell phones were prevalent, and she called me at home one evening on the home phone landline. It was a mutual friend who had urged her to call me. We spent the evening catching up from the previous two years. She had given birth to Jordan Ira in January of 1992, so he was now around eighteen months old. I vividly remember she was giving him a bath when she called. The boyfriend, who was his biological father, abandoned them once he found out Marla was pregnant, which was an enormous blessing from God. If my memory serves me correctly, we had a few more phone calls before I asked her out on a date. That is how it worked when we were young. Spending time talking on the phone was a pretty big deal and was viewed as predating. You spent time on the phone listening to each other's voice, and you got to know that person.

I can remember that first date as if it happened just a few weeks ago. We had dinner at Monterrey's, a local Mexican restaurant. Living in a small town in Tennessee, there was not much to choose from, and Monterrey was one of the few that was a nice, sit-down, casual place to dine. I remember she ordered fajitas, but I don't remember what I had to eat. After dinner, we went to see a movie. Once again, being a small town, there was only one small theater which only had two screens, the Capri. We went to see the first Jurassic Park. I know this was not much of a first date movie, but it was all we had available. I have never been the kind of guy that would try to move real fast in a relationship. What I mean by this statement is that I have never tried to kiss or "make it to second base" on the first date. So after the movie, I took her home, and this beautiful night had ended.

We continued to talk on the phone, and I began to stop by very frequently to see her at work. At that time, she was the assistant manager of the Little Caesar's Pizza store. Our relationship continued to grow. I had taken a job with a construction firm that my cousin was a superintendent of in Harriman, Tennessee. This was a significant drive from where I lived, and for a few weeks, I stayed in a hotel room there close to the jobsite.

One weekend, when I had come back home, I and a friend decided we would get a hotel room in Greeneville. We secured a room at the Charray Hotel, which is still standing but has changed names. This was one way that we could do what we wanted because we didn't have a place of our own at the time. In other words, this is how we would party. This night, however, it was just four people. I had invited Marla, who had brought a mutual friend—Michelle—with her, and my friend David. We were not so much interested in having a party as much as we just wanted a quiet place to hang out without parental interference.

At some point, fairly early in the evening, Michelle wanted to get the two of us alone; so she took David, and they left. This was a small hotel, so there was nothing but one chair and a bed. We were sitting on the bed, just talking and enjoying being with one another, when I leaned over and kissed her. This was the first time we had kissed, and I still, to this day, remember the feeling.

After that night, we began to date each other exclusively. There were many, many obstacles that we managed to overcome. All of them were my fault. I allowed Satan to invade my thoughts with a worldly, fleshly viewpoint. I began to question if I wanted to take on the responsibility of a family right at the onset. I was being utterly selfish with these thoughts, and Marla was not going to play any games with me. I remember her telling me very early that "if I loved her, I would love Jordan."

We actually broke up for a period of time. During this time, which felt like an eternity because Marla was quite a stubborn girl and would not even talk to me during this time, I remember not only missing her but missing Jordan also. This was the moment when God shielded me from my selfishness, and He placed in my heart this overwhelming desire to give Jordan a home. I knew at that point that I wanted to love this little boy like he were my own. I wanted to be his dad!

Marla and I finally managed to patch things up. I am so thankful that she gave me another chance. I felt as if all I did was make a mess out of things. We grew closer and closer, and fell more and more in love as the days passed. I had been given a laboratory job with a local manufacturer during the evening shift. This was a good job, but it didn't pay very well; and having to work the evening shift was not very conducive to a revitalized relationship.

As was the case for most of my youth, I quickly lost patience with this job. I left this position and returned to school, working on a master's degree in education which would allow me to teach. I thought I might want to be a coach primarily, and this was the way to get to that place. But after having spent some time as a substitute teacher and teacher's assistant, I very quickly realized that this was not for me, even with the coaching added in.

As you can see, I was a very impatient young man who had absolutely no plan for his life. I was just trying to get to some place in life, but I had no idea what that place was. I didn't follow through in the area of study that I had chosen out of high school. I had no idea what a career would look like in terms of the business degree that I did manage to complete. And on top of all that, I didn't like the plan B career that I decided upon, which was teaching and coaching. So in all reality, I was a very lost young man. Not only in terms of what I wanted for my life but also in terms of the life I was leading while claiming to be a follower of Jesus Christ.

This brings us to a very crucial point, in terms of the turn that our life—mine and Marla's—took. But more importantly, in terms of how God can take any situation and mold it—like a potter molds a piece of clay, turning it into an unimaginable piece of artwork. Marla and I had continued to grow deeper in love to the point that we started having sex. First of all, I cannot stress enough that this was no trivial matter to Marla after having lived through what she had. Even though Marla was not raised in a Christian home, God had placed a passion in this young lady to seek what was godly and good. The boyfriend had pressured her, against her better judgement, to having sex in the past, for which she was unceremoniously abandoned after having been given this beautiful gift.

Throughout our marriage, we had this same discussion where we both had a great deal of remorse of not having kept ourselves pure for one another. I was way more guilty than she was, having been a male product of the 1980's decade of decadence. But she never had any remorse whatsoever in that little boy whom she loved with all her being. We talked several times about that if she hadn't had made the mistake, this beautiful boy would not exist.

We began talking about eloping early in 1995. This is one of the biggest regrets that I carry with me to this day. The regret of not following through with this plan and having married Marla in the spring of 1995. Right now you might be thinking why. Why would you elope without any real reason, and why is this a big regret for you? Something that we would come to find out later in our marriage was that we both were very fertile people. In the summer of 1995, Marla became pregnant again. Obviously, this time I had given her a gift. But the difference was that I never once had any thought at all of not being her husband and the father to my child. Never ever did it enter my mind that I would leave my responsibilities for any reason.

You might be thinking, *Okay, I can see why you regret not having eloped and being "legal" in getting her pregnant, but why is that still one of your biggest regrets?* The reason is, I could have assumed all the responsibility upon myself by eloping; that would have spared my wife from the ridicule and shame that would later follow being viewed as a promiscuous young lady, having two children out of wedlock. This was not an excessive finger-wagging amount leveled at her, but it was there nonetheless; and it hurt her deeply.

I vividly remember sitting down with her and her dad, and delivering to him the news that she was pregnant. He didn't like me for a quite a while until he realized that I was not going to do the same thing the other guy had done, which was leave. I did protect her from the reaction that my mother had when I told her, by myself, of the situation. I so wish I could have spared her this hurt by being courageous and marrying her the moment we began discussing taking this step.

But here is the first point I would like to make by this personal history review of how we started our marriage: even when you make decisions which are contrary to the plans that God had for you, He will take your mess and make something beautiful out of it. He will mold and shape your life to get to the place that is far greater than anything you could have imagined. And if you remove the thoughts of how badly you failed, you will be able to see the unbelievable magnificence that is placed in front of you.

First, this is not the plan either of us had for what our life would look like. And second, this is definitely not how either of us thought our marriages would begin. But my God can take the messiest of earthly situations, just as He did so many times throughout Scripture, and make them breathtakingly beautiful to display His magnificent grace.

CHAPTER 2

Twenty-Three Years in the Blink of an Eye

I don't like to spend very much time talking about myself and my past, but I believe it establishes context and some key pieces of truth. The truth that all human beings are flawed, and many of us don't start out our lives or our marriages with the nice, fairly tell beginnings. We have plans, and sometimes we mess those plans up. In today's society, it has become very hard to forget the past mistakes and instead focus on the lessons those mistakes teach us. Today, Satan's forces have used social media to their full advantage by not only keeping the focus on the past but also by eliminating any forgiveness for those past mistakes. We see this played out in the lives of public figures who have some individual, or the media, dig up some past comment on social media and use it to cause damage and, in some instances, ruin the public figure's life.

As I stated in Chapter 1, Marla and I were a very fertile couple, and apparently I only produce males. We have four sons: Jordan, Andrew, Jacob, and Dallas Aron. We had spent the majority of our adult life in Greeneville, Tennessee. I ultimately landed at a very good place to work in the nuclear industry in Erwin, Tennessee, and we settled down into the routine of raising our sons. You know, the usual things such as school, sports, and family traditions.

In 2010, I was blocked for a promotion where I worked and decided I was going to see what other opportunities were out there in my field. I was offered a job as a contractor, which would move us to Paducah, Kentucky. And we believed it was a good time to make a change because Jordan was just graduating high school, and Andrew was finishing middle school; so I accepted. We began preparing to leave East Tennessee where we had lived our entire lives.

Although the timing was good, this was still very difficult, especially for Marla, because of leaving Jordan behind in Tennessee. He was to begin college the fall of 2010 at East Tennessee State University, and we were leaving in June; so it didn't make sense for him to come with us. He stayed behind with grandparents and worked through the summer. But as we discovered looking back, it was the best decision we made. We grew exponentially closer by being away from family and friends. We only had each other to rely on and had to lean on each other greatly more than we ever had to before. But it was not only limited to us; the boys grew so much closer to each other as well.

Things continued to change, as is always the case in life. Whether you have major changes or small changes, change is the only constant in life. After a year, I changed employers in the area. And as my luck would have it, after a few months the Department of Energy contracting company I was with had a major contract fall through, and they were ceasing operations. So here I am looking for another job again. I tried so hard to stay within a decent distance of Paducah so we would not have to move again. We had a beautiful house, the best house we had lived in since we were married. But that was not God's plan. I was offered a job with the company that was building the two new nuclear reactors just below Augusta, Georgia. I tried to find any excuse not to take the job, but everything I was coming up with was quickly dismissed. I even requested what I thought was a salary that would have been laughed at, but the company did not even hesitate.

After months of trying to not to move from our new home, I had to talk myself into getting excited about the thoughts of being involved in a project that hadn't been done in over thirty years. And I will admit that it didn't take long for me to become excited about this career move. But my sons were not happy about it at all, especially

Andrew. For him this would mean three high schools in three years. So needless to say, I was not a popular father at the time.

We did a much more thorough job in researching the Augusta, Georgia, area than we had previously done with Paducah, Kentucky. There were far greater opportunities in Augusta as opposed to Paducah as well, especially in the secondary education arena. We had actually had a small preview of the area prior to 2012 when I was employed with Nuclear Fuel Services in Tennessee. NFS had some small contract projects at the Savannah River Nuclear Site, which is just across the river from Augusta. So we had looked briefly into the area before, but I was never offered a transfer to come to the project at the time.

I had started work on April 29, 2012, at the Vogtle Units 3 and 4 new nuclear reactor construction site. But Marla and the boys stayed behind in Paducah to finish out the school semester. Andrew was completing his sophomore year in high school, and Jacob was completing his seventh-grade year in middle school. They followed down to Augusta in June after I had secured a rental house, and the moving company had packaged and loaded up our belongings. Marla oversaw that process in Kentucky and left once the moving company had loaded. We met with the high school football coach at Augusta Christian during June of 2012. Mr. Keith Walton was his name, and he is a very strong Christian gentleman who is now in full-time ministry. From the moment we met with him, we knew this was where our sons were going to attend school.

We settled into our new home in Augusta, Georgia. Marla absolutely loved the area, primarily because her uncle had lived just a few minutes from Augusta and she had very fond memories of visiting them when she was young. Incidentally she originally had aspirations of attending the University of Georgia when she graduated high school, but God had different plans for her. Andrew worked hard and earned a starting position as offensive guard on the Augusta Christian High School Football team.

Jacob also was a hardworking gifted athlete at Augusta Christian. Marla continued to homeschool the youngest son, Dallas Aron. She began to seek out a homeschool cooperative group, and God brought these wonderful ladies into our lives through this effort. These ladies were forming a new homeschool cooperative group, and after interviewing many other groups, Marla was thrilled to be invited and involved with this new group, the Sojourners.

The year 2012 was one of the most memorable years of my life. You must remember that neither of us had moved anywhere in our life. I spent forty years in East Tennessee, and she spent thirty-seven. Our family ties to the area runs very deep. For me it was over seven generations in the East Tennessee area, and for Marla it was at least four generations. So to have to move again in such a short period of time, after a monumental decision of leaving Tennessee in the first place, was a big shock to our lives. But with so much unrest, strife, and complete chaos that was taking place, God gave us the most unbelievably beautiful outcome through it all.

As the school year began and football season started, things began to feel like they had never felt before. Even being new to the school and the area, we felt welcome, and those nights at the Augusta Christian football field were comforting in a way that I can't describe. The families at Augusta Christian were very hospitable and receiving of new families into the mix. I made friends with the other fathers, and Marla, who was a reserved individual by nature, was welcomed and made friends with the other players' mothers.

The team that year was an extremely talented team. Many of the senior players had played together for several years, and other highly talented players had been added to the mix, including my son Andrew. The team began the year off with a tough team and managed to pull out a tight victory. This, I believe, set the tone for the remainder of the season. Each game, the team continued to progress and improve. Ultimately, they went undefeated and won a state championship.

God provided this blessing to us out of something that began as an unwanted change, which was out of our control, and at the time felt as if it were some form of punishment. For Andrew, it was an answer to his prayer and gave him something that he would not have been able to accomplish in Kentucky. Outside of sports, the school itself was an amazing gift that gave Andrew and Jacob an excellent Christ-centered education.

As the 2012–2013 school year came to a close, we began to really settle into our new home. After this fabulous mountaintop experience, we descended into the everyday life and completely embraced the area God had brought us. After attending many local churches in search of the congregation that we felt we would fit into the best, we landed at Warren Baptist Church. Albeit a much larger church than anything we had experienced in the past, we felt we could grow both spiritually and socially in our new home.

After some time had passed, we both sought out ways we could begin serving at Warren. I believed we had served quite well in the outreach ministry in Kentucky, so I really wanted to maintain that momentum and not fall back into the realm of simply attending church. Marla began feeling a strong call to teach elementary-age young girls and began helping in that ministry. I, on the other hand, didn't quite know how I wanted to serve, but I started out by coaching soccer and basketball in the Upward league at Warren. Primarily, I felt that I needed to be very involved with our youngest son, Dallas Aron. I felt as if I had not given him the same attention at his age that I had given the other boys. We had such a wonderful time together during these years that I coached him. He was still in the elementary age group but was about to change to the middle school age group.

I remember starting to get involved with the middle school ministry group when our friends, the Passmores, were wanting to transition out of the middle school ministry because both of their sons had moved up to high school. This is when I was approached to teach the middle school boys youth group. I began with the sixth-grade boys' group because that was the grade Dallas was in at the time. This was a wonderful group of young men, and I really enjoyed being able to share my knowledge of the Scripture with them. I moved up with them each year until they were heading to the high school ministry. This is where I stopped teaching them because I felt they needed a different perspective on the Scripture than just my own. I transitioned into working the audiovisual equipment for the middle school and remained in that position until the worst thing to happen in my life occurred.

This is the point where I begin to describe the reason for me feeling led to write this book in the first place. This is the worst and darkest time in my life to date. It began in 2016. I had accepted a promotion while I was working at Vogtle to a position which required that I work in the corporate office in Charlotte, North Carolina. Incidentally, this is one of the biggest regrets that I now carry with me, being away from our home during the week. I would leave early on Monday morning and stay until Thursday afternoon. I missed so much time with Marla during these two years. I do certainly wish that I would have really grasped the fragility of our existence. That at any minute, we might be called home. There are no guarantees that we will take another breath. But many of us, including myself at that time, live as if we have a guarantee that we will make it to a certain age.

I was in Charlotte when my father began having some problems with a sciatic nerve. He had surgery but was having some complications after the surgery. He just wasn't his robust self who had never been in a hospital in his life for any length of time. I was called home because Dad had been admitted to the hospital for some problems. Marla and the boys loaded up and met me back in our hometown, Greeneville, Tennessee. The hospital had performed some procedure, but Dad had a major infection and was not coming out of it.

As usual the fantastic, amazing industry that is the United States healthcare industry said there was nothing more they could do. Dad had actually been in the hospital for a few days, and I had seen him the previous weekend, I believe. He just didn't look himself at that time. Dad was always in a good mood and would joke a lot, but this time, he seemed distant and preoccupied, as if to say that he was tired and ready to go to his heavenly home.

Marla met me at the hospital, and she and I actually spent the night in the bed next to my father's in that hospital room. I vividly remember all night wondering how Dad was still alive because he sounded like he was breathing underwater. Each breath would gurgle so loudly that I just couldn't understand how he was getting any oxygen at all. By the way, I don't remember any hospital staff coming in at any time during the night to check on him. They had written him off and was simply waiting on him to die. This was January 28, 2017.

The next evening, January 29, 2017, at 7:15 p.m.—with me, Marla, my sons, my mother, my aunt, and two of my cousins standing by the bed—we watched my father take his last breath here on Earth. Although, being a child, you realize that one day your parents will pass away, it still hits hard.

My dad and I were very close. Although you might not know it by being around us, as we didn't talk to each other a great deal. This man was my mentor, my example of what it meant to be a Christian. He taught me more than this world could offer, and he rarely spoke words to do it. I was blessed by being given the strength to speak during his memorial service, and here is what I wrote and shared with the congregation:

"Please forgive me, as I am about to break most, if not all, of the rules of public speaking by reading to you what I want to say. I have been thinking about this for some time now and decided that although I spent time as a member of the Gideons, having stood in this very pulpit, I don't know if I could make it through this without writing it out and not making eye contact with you, the audience. I appreciate each of you coming out today to honor how my father had touched your life in some way. I could stand here and tell you of many stories through the forty-seven years that I have shared with my dad.

"I could tell you stories that many of you were a part of in some way, whether you were a part of my large extended family who shared in many get-togethers or a schoolmate who shared in numerous sporting escapades. But I will not bore you with rehashing stories you would know well, nor tell you of times when I would lie on the kitchen floor underneath some newspapers thinking that I was hidden while I waited on Dad to walk through the door from work. What I want to share with you today is a story that I believe Dad would want all of you to hear and understand, although he would most likely not have been able to share it with you himself.

"Dad had a tough childhood growing up and did not have a keen understanding of how to communicate love. Now pay close attention to the word I just used, which is communicate. As I heard many times last night, God had blessed Bill Gardner with an over-abundance of compassion, gentleness, and an extraordinary ability of how to demonstrate love no matter who you were or what your status was in life. Dad never met a stranger and was so understanding that it sometimes cost him in some way, but that never changed his character.

"Growing up, I never questioned that Dad loved me and was proud of me, although I cannot remember ever hearing those words come out of his mouth. Mom, however, was the opposite and would tell me she loved me while busting my behind around the yard with a hickory switch. Once I became a teenager, Dad and I each had basically come to the mutual understanding that we both just *knew* that we loved each other, and being men, neither of us still ever uttered the words.

"Now let's move forward to 1995 and the introduction of a beautiful young woman and child into the mix. Yes, I heard the collective eyebrows raise. That young woman was his new daughter-in-law, Marla, and his new grandson Jordan. One of Marla's love languages is words of affirmation. If you have not heard of the book *The Five Love Languages*, I highly recommend you find a copy, as it is very helpful in understanding how we show love to one another. But as I said, one way to exhibit love to Marla is to tell her. Thus began my education into how to show love in different ways depending on the recipient, and as you may speculate, each of our sons has a different primary love language.

"Once we were married, Marla would continue to tell Dad that she loved him until he responded. This would sometimes take several times before he would finally give in and tell her. So it became a badge of honor for her to get Dad to respond. Consequently, she would also continue to prod me that I should tell Dad more often even though we had formed the 'understanding.' To further add to this equation, you had the introduction of more grandsons who also would tell their papa they loved him and would jump in his lap or ask to be carried. This became commonplace in our household.

"In 2010, I received and accepted a job offer in Western Kentucky, so we moved. And it was the first time we couldn't be home frequently. Every time we would come in to visit, Dad would tear up as we were leaving and sometimes could not watch us pull out of the driveway. But although he had made a lot of improvement, he still was not very forthcoming in being the first to say the words. I had become much more vocal through the years. I am sure many of you are looking at each other right now and rolling your eyes, thinking, *Since when has Dallas Gardner had a problem with opening his mouth?*

"Persistence erodes away fear, and tenacity yields results. The past five years, Dad would tell all of us that he loved us and was proud of us. To the point that during a phone call with him not too long ago, as we were getting off the phone, Dad was the first to quickly tell me that he loved me. I was momentarily taken aback but realized he had learned the lesson well. To the point that Dad had confided in Marla that he admired me and the relationship that I have with my boys. No, Dad, I learned from the best!

"I have heard more times than I care to count the words, 'I am sorry for your loss.' I began to ponder these words. *Loss*, by its definition, denotes there is something that you will not get back. Yes, I will not reclaim time with Dad that I wish I could have done things better or more often. Obviously, I will not get back the time between now and when I leave this world. But I can tell you with unwavering faith and utmost certainty that I will see my Dad again one day. On that day, I will be escorted by my earthly father and mother to stand face-to-face with Jesus Christ in whom they both placed their faith and in whom, by their example, my life has been redeemed. To that end I say, thank you, Lord, for godly parents. And I love you, Mom… I love you, Dad." As you see, Marla had an enormous impact upon my Dad.

After the passing of my dad, we came back to Augusta and finished the school year. This was the year that Jacob Noah, our third son, was graduating high school from Augusta Christian. Not to mention for three years, we had been involved with the China Project Hope and had accommodated a Chinese exchange student, Tenjuen Gao. His American adopted name was David. David was graduating this year also, and Marla had been very instrumental in getting this young man into the University of Nebraska. Graduation took place in May of 2017, and it was a wonderful celebration we all shared in.

* * * * *

But on July 5, 2017, Marla woke up and could not stand upright due to a pain in her abdomen. We both new that it was most likely appendicitis, so we headed to the urgent care clinic. The urgent care clinic advised that we needed to go directly to the emergency room at a local hospital, as there was nothing they could do at the clinic. So we went to the nearest hospital, which was Doctors Hospital in Augusta, Georgia.

When they got around to seeing Marla, they did confirm that it was appendicitis and brought in a doctor by the name of Buchanan. She informed us that the way that the industry treats appendicitis today is by inserting a tube to drain off the infection into a collection bag on the outside of the person before going in to remove the appendix. We were told this would eliminate the infection from getting into other areas of her abdomen in removing the appendix. They proceeded to take her into the operating room and inserted the tube to drain the infection.

For the next six weeks, she had a few follow-up appointments, and at one point they brought her back into the hospital to adjust the tube because the infection had stopped draining. This is the point where the hospital punctured her colon in trying to insert the tube into her appendix a second time. From everything that I have been told, her body was doing an excellent job of fighting this appendix problem and had walled off her appendix with this hard shell to encapsulate the infection. So they had a hard time getting the tube inserted into the appendix and, in doing so, had punctured her colon going into the appendix.

During one of the many visits, the doctor had informed us that they were going to need to remove the right side of her colon along with the appendix because of what had been proceeding. Fast-forward to the day of the surgery in which they removed the right part of Marla's colon and appendix, the doctor informed us that it had been cancerous but that she felt they had gotten well over the margins necessary to remove all the cancer.

This hit us both hard. But I believe we processed the information very differently. I believe Marla felt that she had just been given a death sentence, while I was confident that she would get through this because she was doing well and she was so much stronger than she gave herself credit. I have never been an overly optimistic person, but for whatever reason, immediately after all the surgery and consultation, I was sure that Marla was going to be just fine.

* * * * *

Around October of 2017, Marla went in for a positron emission tomography (PET) scan to determine if any cancer remained after the surgery. She had also been provided an oncologist to take her case from Doctors Hospital. Once the results from the scan came in, there was a quarter-sized spot on her liver, and this was all the scan showed at that time. Marla had been scared her whole life about her health and safety. And the entire time that we were together, that was still the case.

Even in her own admission, this went back to an episode when she was three years old and her urethra tube that was too small. In a procedure to stretch and widen the tube, the doctor cut her artery. But it wasn't until later, when she and her sister were playing, that she started to bleed internally and almost died. This was extremely traumatic not only for her but for Mary, her mother.

Mary was fiercely protective of Marla after that event. With that being said, she was very afraid of undergoing chemotherapy because she felt she would not survive the treatment. Due to the track record with the so-called medical profession, I tended to agree with her. This is when she began to research alternative therapies and other forms of treatments, such as diet and acupuncture, to stop or eliminate this cancerous spot on her liver. She was very determined to do anything and everything nonconventional she could to heal herself.

I was very much in her corner, but to the point that I was somewhat in a state of denial about what was happening. I firmly believed that this was very small and that she was going to be just fine. She ultimately was referred to a lady in the next county north of us who had a small alternative therapy practice. This lady was a registered nurse and had been married to a physician, so she seemed to be one who could be trusted. The biggest thing she wanted to do for Marla was ozone therapy. This is where the blood is taken from her body, is infused with oxygen that contains a third electron or O_3, and is put back into her body. The concept is that most living things cannot survive in an oxygen-enriched environment.

Having been a chemistry major in college, this seemed to make sense, but I had not devoted much time nor effort into studying for myself the perceived benefits of this treatment. I have since read a little about it by a medical doctor who wrote a book discussing many alternative treatments as to whether they had merit and those that were not backed by any data substantiating their validity. Ozone was one that, according to this doctor, had very little data backing up the claims. This doctor also cited some research that believed ozone therapy actually accelerated cancer growth.

Needless to say, after I read this book, I was very angry at the thoughts that I didn't do anything to research and help my wife make informed decisions. She was too trusting of those she knew who recommended these treatments. I was too caught up in my work problems, and things that did not matter in the least bit during this time. I really failed her and will not forgive myself for being shortsighted and selfish.

The holidays during that year were very much not normal. It was not a good holiday season at all, and looking back, it was most likely a precursor to prepare me for what lay ahead. Marla was scheduled to have a follow-up PET scan at the end of December. Because of this and the Chinese exchange student we still had at the time, she did not go with us back to our hometown in Tennessee for

Christmas. The exchange student was not David that was mentioned earlier but a different student, whose American name was Leo. He was not at all like David. He was an entitled little brat. During the holidays, David also wanted to come back to visit from Nebraska primarily because they couldn't afford for him to go back to China for a couple of weeks. But he did help with the communication issues with Leo, who could not speak English very well.

This Christmas season was very off. At the time, we kind of went through the motions, and I was not thinking too much about the circumstances; but it still just didn't feel right at all. It was depressing both for myself, our sons, and Marla's mother and sister. Additionally, during the months of November and December, she began having pain in her back. The medical establishment never really gave a clear indication as to what it was but prescribed her physical therapy. At some point, there was an indication that it might be a disc problem in her back. She remained in this state of discomfort for quite a while beginning in December.

All of us but Marla have birthdays in the month of January. My and Jacob's day is January 13, Dallas Aron is January 16, Jordan is January 18, and Andrew's is February 2. He missed it by two days. I don't recall anything out of the ordinary for January. Celebrating everyone's birthday has always somewhat been an extension of the holidays, and this year was not different. I don't recall anything out of the ordinary during the month of January 2018. Even the first part of February came and went without anything to speak of, but then came February 20, 2018. I will never be able to erase from my memory the events of that day.

To start the day, Marla received a message from Jordan and Lindsey that they had finally been notified about a possible adoption and were given around two hours to get to the local hospital because the little boy, who was the one being adopted, was about to be born. This was a long-awaited blessing that my son and his wife had been waiting for about four years or more. However, as the day progressed, Marla just kept getting sicker and sicker. To the point that she was shaking violently all over.

We were completely clueless as to what was happening. But it became severe, and I almost had to carry her to the car and get her to the hospital emergency room. There she was placed on the highest priority and was rushed into a room. The area where they had performed the colonoscopy had perforated, and Marla was septic to the point of death. How she survived this day, I will never know. Other than she was at least meant to see her grandson, who was being born at the exact same moment that she herself was standing at the precipice of heaven, this was the beginning of the utmost amount of uncertainty and confusion that I have ever been a part of for my entire life.

After the hospital had stabilized her with antibiotics and were able to stop the sepsis from getting worse, she was admitted to continue reducing the septic condition and to assess what had happened. This is where the myriad of doctors began to be brought in, reminiscent of the clown car at a circus. Scan after scan and proposed diagnosis after diagnosis soon followed in ever-evolving succession. The most disturbing aspect was the somewhat contradictory opinions coming from the different specialists. Most notably was the infectious specialist who was almost certain that the spot on her liver was not cancer but was a pocket of infection because it was too uniformly round.

This began the roller coaster ride that went on for the next several months. This really gave Marla a huge confidence boost to her mental state. She was so excited to receive this information, and it lifted her spirits tremendously. The doctors proceeded to take a sample of the spot on her liver, and to our dismay, it came back as showing markers of cancer; but this was not communicated as a definitive answer. There was still this sort of disbelief from the doctors that this was the case.

She finally got to the place where they released her to go home. She ramped up the ozone therapy treatments along with other treatments, such as acupuncture and nutritional therapy. Around April, Marla went back to Tennessee to a dentist in Knoxville to have some of her teeth removed because of ongoing infections that these had created. She had learned, during all this, that dental problems, especially root canals, created a huge burden upon a person's immune system. Being that she had half of her thyroid removed some years ago due to a goiter, she was very concerned about overburdening her immune system.

We began seeking out other nontraditional medical professionals who might offer some other types of treatment. We researched a doctor in Charlotte and another clinic in Myrtle Beach. I had a former coworker who lives in Myrtle Beach, so we would have had some assistance with staying there during this time if we would have been able to start there.

This went on from March to June of 2018. There were doctors who came and dropped off their opinion and left. No one really wanted to help Marla except the oncologist, who wanted to pump her full of battery acid to kill everything inside her and—oh, just by chance—maybe the cancer cells also. In the meantime, there were visits from relatives and from her new grandson. There are pictures of her and Oliver taken from her hospital bed. She would light up every time she saw this little guy. She still was dealing with pain both in her abdomen area and also in her back, and was beginning to lose a lot of weight. I chalked this up to the colonoscopy and her greatly reduced appetite. But I will find out that I was very wrong.

During this entire time, our third son, Jacob, was waiting to be sent off to basic military training for the Air Force National Guard. He had joined in 2017 and was sworn in November 2017, of which I went with him for the ceremony. Due to being in the National Guard, he was having to wait for slots to open up, as most were filled by full-time active-duty members. He finally received his orders and was scheduled to depart for San Antonio on July 31, 2018.

The month of July 2018 is the point that things deteriorated extremely rapidly. Almost too fast to keep up with mentally. On July 19, 2018, Marla began to vomit for no real apparent reason. I don't recall what I was doing at the time, but I came in the house to find her on the back deck vomiting, sobbing, trembling, and panicking severely. I picked her up, cleaned her up, and tried my best to calm her down. I can still see the look of terror on her face as she seemed to know that something was really wrong.

We left immediately for the emergency room, where they were very slow in getting her some attention. Finally I remember having a couple of ER doctors come in during this visit and, in essence, ask us—more specifically, Marla—if her affairs were in order. I was dumbfounded by this, as we had not really been asked these questions until now. But they were not telling us much more than that. Ultimately, Marla had a partial blockage in her bowels, and this was causing a backup in her system to the point that her body instinctively started vomiting to eliminate the waste.

After admitting her to the hospital and running a battery of tests, yet again a different doctor was assigned to the case. This was primarily because the previous doctor had left University Hospital. The doctor assigned actually went to the same church that we had attended for some time now, and his son also attended Augusta Christian and played football. But he offered nothing but condolences as in his estimation. Marla's liver was almost engulfed in the cancer, and there was "nothing" he could do. One thing that was presented was to put in an ileostomy. This was a bypass of her bowels and, similar to a colostomy, would be placed in the side of her abdomen to allow for her to continue to take in nutrition and expel waste. This procedure was actually performed by a visiting surgeon from the hospital in the Fort Gordon Army base nearby.

While she was performing the surgery, she looked around to try and assess Marla's situation. In this surgeon's opinion, Marla's cancer on her liver looked to be more to one side, and she advised us to seek out better specialists on the subject at either Emory Hospital in Atlanta or MD Anderson in Houston, Texas. Additionally, during this time in the hospital, we were visited by and advised to obtain hospice services. For me, this was not clear why because the real reason was not readily being given. I was under the impression that this was to assist Marla, but actually it was to only provide her comfort, as they simply assisted in ushering you from this life as painlessly as possible.

After we had been educated and trained on how to clean and change her ostomy bag and she had been stabilized, we again were sent home. Once some of the dust settled, Marla immediately began to schedule a visit and request that all her records be sent to Emory Hospital just outside of Atlanta to their cancer unit and one of the doctors there. Painfully for everyone, but especially for Marla, was that Jacob had to leave for bootcamp on July 31, 2018.

It was a very somber morning when we woke up, and everyone, especially Jacob, was in a very depressed mood. There was not much talking as we drove Jacob to the airport. All of us went to see him off, and my precious wife was in a wheelchair because she was so weak from everything that had just transpired. There are pictures that we have from the airport that day, and I can't look at them because you can see it in Marla's eyes, and also in Jacob's eyes, that both of them believed they would not see each other again.

I was trying to have enough courage for everyone during this time and was in a state of denial, I suppose, because I had faith that somehow Marla would come out of this period healed in some way. Jacob was on his way and would tell me later that it was the hardest day he ever faced when he had to leave with his mother in the state she was in. Although we were not supposed to do this while under hospice care, we scheduled an appointment with the doctor at Emory Hospital for August 24, 2018.

* * * * *

The months of July and August of 2018 were the absolute most terrible months that I have lived through or possibly will ever live through. The majority of the time, Marla was having to take so much pain medication that she was hardly coherent. She would fall asleep constantly, simply sitting in her chair or the couch. She would be in so much pain when she had to sit on the toilet, and several times I would carry her little body to the bed or bathroom because she was so frail. The hospice had brought in a bed that would incline both in the torso and leg sections along with some other pieces of medical equipment for her to use, such as an oxygen machine for her to get enough oxygen while she slept or whenever she felt she needed it. Most of the time she slept with it on, as it blended in with the fan that we always slept with during our marriage.

August 24, 2018, was the day the appointment with the cancer center at Emory University in Atlanta, Georgia, was scheduled. I took the day off where I was working with Westinghouse still to take her to the appointment. That was a day I care not to remember. She continued to need a wheelchair because she simply could not walk very far because of her weakened state.

We had driven the 2006 Toyota Camry that I used to go back and forth to work mostly because it was smaller but still had ample room for her to recline and relax, plus transport the wheelchair. We arrived, and I pushed her into the facility where we checked in; and she had to fill out some additional paperwork. We eventually were called back into an examination room where we were first met by a younger physician who, I believe, was a sort of apprentice to the more seasoned physician who ultimately came in to speak with us regarding Marla's condition. There was also in the room a much younger lady who might have been a student. I do not know, as some details have been erased from my memory.

The older, more seasoned doctor came in and began to explain to us some things he had seen just in reviewing her medical records to date. The first thing he said was, this type of cancer did not respond to chemotherapy, of which everyone at University Hospital and Doctors Hospital in Augusta were pushing upon Marla to undergo. The next thing he said was the type of cancer was very aggressive. And finally, he asked us if we knew that she had a tumor behind her stomach. After being told this about her stomach, I was immediately furious because absolutely no one had mentioned this to date.

On August 24, 2018, a full six months after her colonoscopy had ruptured and almost a full year since we were first told that there were cancer cells in her system after the appendectomy, we were told about a tumor behind her stomach. I cannot begin to explain to you the rage with the medical system in this country I was feeling after that piece of news. This also explained why her back had been hurting since November of 2017; why she had lost her ability to take in food and nutrients; why the right side of her kidneys had a tube impingement that caused the doctors to go in and insert a stint into her kidney tube, which did nothing to alleviate the swelling in her kidneys; and ultimately why her bowels had an obstruction, causing her to vomit because the food was being bottlenecked and could not progress further. I cannot explain to you the absolute and utter loss of any amount of respect for the medical profession as a whole.

As you would imagine, the doctor may as well have punched my wife in the stomach with all the force he could muster because that is what this news invariably did to her. And on top of all that, on our way driving back home from Atlanta, our son Jacob, who had been in boot camp for almost a month, called to talk with us. Looking back on that moment, I realize now how unbelievably strong my wife was. Even in the midst of the most devastating news anyone could be given, she spoke to our son in the most encouraging way.

She lifted his spirits, and as she had done since the day he was born, she told him how special and proud she was of him. She never once indicated to him that she was utterly destroyed by the news we were just given. It was the absolute, most remarkable thing I believe I have witnessed in my life. Some things in life are seared into your memory, and for me, this is one of those moments.

* * * * *

We arrived back home, and as you would guess, Marla was extremely exhausted from that day. I honestly can't remember much once we were back home. I believe the news must have drove me into a deep state of denial that I was not fully aware of at that time. We returned to where we had been prior to the appointment at Emory, which was just getting through each day together, and I returned to work. I really wish I would have taken more time off from work to be with her. It is another in a long line of regrets that I have during these years of my life.

There had been events which were taking place and had been going on for quite some time at this point. The Warren Church Sunday school class we attended had been bringing meals for us. The ladies in the homeschool cooperative group were coming by, as was those individuals we were close to at Augusta Christian Schools. Several people would come and visit with Marla, bringing her anything she desired at that time. They would sit and talk with her even though at times she was in a drug-induced, foggy state from the pain medication.

The gentleman who was assigned to Marla's case from the hospice organization would visit to check in on her and make sure she had the medication or medical devices that were needed. All these things made our home feel very different than the closeness we always shared as a family through the years. We always made it a top priority to eat dinner together as a family, and I believe this was one of, if not the primary, reasons our family was so tight-knit and shared a deep closeness. Now these times became fleeting, as Marla could not come to the table, much less cook for her family. Something she prided herself in her entire life was cooking for her men each and every night.

Marla's health really dropped dramatically after August 24 to the point that I was advised by the hospice nurse to call the air force and get Jacob a pass to come home and visit with his mother while he still had the chance. I immediately began the process of getting the message to him via the Red Cross and sending in the necessary paperwork to get him some time before there was no more time to be had with his mother. The process actually worked very well, and my sincerest thanks to the Red Cross organization for what they do in times like these.

Jacob was allowed to leave and fly back home for about one week, September 3 through 6 if I remember correctly. Marla's demeanor immediately changed for the better. Looking back on this time period, she was probably "rallying" as many have said happens right before the end. But she was so happy and cheerful to see her son and spend time with him. I believe this, in turn, caused me to have even more denial to the state of her health because I just knew that somehow, someway, she was going to get through this battle. Jacob had to return to Lackland Air Force Base in San Antonio, Texas, around the sixth of September 2018.

Several months prior, we had made plans and had purchased airline tickets in anticipation of flying out to watch Jacob graduate from Air Force Basic Military Training on September 20–21, 2018.

We both realized that Marla potentially might not be able to travel, but both of us had a very positive outlook about the possibility. As you have read, the realization came to pass, and Marla was in no way able to travel that far, especially by air. She was not only in a very weakened state due to the cancer but she also was very afraid of heights.

As I mentioned earlier, she had been in such a wonderful state the week that Jacob was home to visit, but the week after he left to return to boot camp, she immediately started to get even worse than before his visit. I was extremely hesitant to leave her to go see our son graduate. As you might have guessed, I was very much torn in two by this situation. I absolutely did not want to leave her, but I also did not want to abandon my son, leaving him by himself completely during a very momentous occasion. It was actually Marla who begged me to go and be with Jacob. As you will see in a minute, I believe I know why.

Marla's mother, Mary Miller, came down from Tennessee to stay with Marla and Andrew, my second oldest son. We had decided that my youngest son, Dallas Aron, would take Marla's place on the trip. On Wednesday, September 18, 2018, Dallas Aron and I left for San Antonio, Texas. I was very unsettled the whole time. The trip was horrible, as we had quite a time changing passengers from Marla to my son, but that is irrelevant.

We arrived in the evening in San Antonio and got settled into our hotel room. The next day, Thursday, September 20, 2018, we went to the base, checked in, and waited for the ceremony to begin. It was a very nice day, and we had a memorable time with Jacob, watching all the festivities and honors being handed out. I was very proud of our son. I texted some pictures back to Mary who showed Marla, and Marla at least was able to comment on how handsome Jacob was in the picture. Jacob was still not allowed to leave the base on Thursday evening; however, we did spend the day together on the base, mostly at the food court area but also driving around the base. It might have been fairly uneventful as a whole, but it was still a very good day under the circumstances.

The next day, Friday, September 21, 2021, started very nice and relaxed. Dallas and I went down to get some breakfast in the hotel, which was not very much at all. We then left and went back to the base for the second day, which was the more formal day for the boot camp graduation. This was the marching day and the day that the awards were presented during the rank-and-file session. The ceremony concluded, and afterwards, the soldiers were allowed to leave the base with their families. Dallas, Jacob, and I left the base and traveled to downtown San Antonio to get some lunch and see what we could find to visit while we were here. I don't really remember much of this time in great detail because of what was happening. But to the best of my recollection, we were not scheduled to fly back to Georgia until Sunday, October 23, 2018.

We ended up eating at a very nice restaurant in the heart of San Antonio, and afterwards, we visited the Alamo and took in that magnificent historical site. We were not in much of a hurry, but we finished up touring the Alamo by midafternoon and returned to our hotel to relax for a bit. Early evening, we left the hotel and drove around near the base looking for a place to eat. We stopped at a Texas barbecue restaurant that I believe was a buffet-style venue. It was a good place to eat, but nothing that was overly impressive for the renowned Texas style barbecue.

After we ate, it was still early in the evening—approximately 6:30 p.m., I believe—we decided to drive around and see if there was something we could do to occupy some time before going back to the hotel for the night. We found a shopping mall and decided to go in simply to walk around for a bit. As we pulled into the mall parking lot, somewhere around 7:10 p.m., we walked toward the entrance. We had just got to the entry door of the mall when my phone rang: it was my sister-in-law, Misty.

My heart immediately sank because I knew she would not be calling if there wasn't something wrong. And as I suspected, so began the worst ending to the worst day of my life. She was telling me that my beautiful wife's eyes had set in place and that she was struggling to breathe. I absolutely cannot express to you the sheer and utter devastation that hit me like a sledgehammer to the abdomen. I let Jacob and Dallas know there was something wrong, and we immediately turned around and headed back to the vehicle. In my mind, I was going to get back to the hotel as fast as I could to FaceTime Misty.

As we were driving back to the hotel, I didn't get very far when something told me to go ahead and FaceTime right then, so I did. I watched through a waterfall of tears and pleas my wife struggle to breathe with the hospice nurse and my sister-in-law in the background trying to console me. I have no idea how we managed not to hit something or another vehicle that day other than God took over driving for me that evening.

Jacob wanted to go immediately back to the air base and petition to be allowed to leave because of the situation, and there in the parking lot of Lackland Air Force Base, I was told my wife drew her last breath. Immediately I was filled with regret that I was not there to hold her hand. To this day, that is my greatest regret. But I believe she did it on purpose, not wanting for me or her youngest son to be there when she took Jesus by the hand and stepped into His presence. I also believe she did not want to leave my son by himself with what all was going on at the time.

Jacob came back to the car and informed us of what he discussed with his superiors and that he would stay on the base that night as we were trying to get the first flight out in the morning. I had been on the phone, while Jacob was talking with his leadership, trying to make arrangements to get on the first flight back to Atlanta the following morning. I don't recall anything that night—how I slept, what we did, or what I was thinking. I was simply in a state of shock, I suppose.

Dallas and I got up very early to get to the airport and through security, around 3:00 a.m. central time. There was very little, if any, talk this morning. I do remember getting some food while we waited for the boarding call. We had a very indistinct flight back to Atlanta and made our way to our vehicle, which was in a parking garage next to the airport. I seemed to recall being very impatient with traffic that morning, but that is not really out of character for me.

I do seem to recall this looming feeling of dread the entire way back from Atlanta to Augusta. I apparently was on autopilot due to being in a state of shock for the most part. I don't recall very many details at all from this time in my life. It is all shrouded in a cloud of denial and shock.

I arrived back at our home around twelve o'clock noon, eastern time. Marla's sister and mother were there along with my oldest son and his family. I walked into the house, and to my utter amazement, the house had been returned to normal-looking, just like it did before the hospice came and brought the adjustable bed along with the other pieces of equipment. All the things that were there from the past three months were gone. This was a shock to my system because it was as if I had dreamed all of this, with the exception that my beautiful wife was not there physically any longer.

I still, to this day, think about the impact this had upon me mentally. It's as if I missed out on something, albeit the absolute most painful experience I could ever imagine. But I felt a surge of sheer remorse that I was not there alongside her as she has been by my side for over twenty years. The torment of this feeling was brutal. The second-guessing of the decision to travel out to be with Jacob during his graduation from the air force training quickly consumed me. Obviously, there was a river of tears yet to be shed. Without my Savior, Jesus Christ, I have no idea how I would have navigated this time.

So on September 21, 2018, at 7:28 p.m. eastern time, the absolute, most beautiful period of my life came to a close. Two years shy of our twenty-fifth wedding anniversary, which cut me to the core as well. I do not nor would not wish this feeling upon my worst enemy. And I cannot, for the life of me, understand how people throw away relationships and marriages as easily as they do.

Of course, we had downtimes, not-so-good times, but the mountaintops were amazingly breathtaking! The day-to-day things are those that I miss the most and encourage everyone who may read this: to stop worrying about the small things in life and live. Marla said over and over, during the last two months of her life here on Earth, that all she wanted to do was live! To be there for each new moment of her son's lives, to be there for her grandchildren, and most importantly to be there walking side by side with me in the twilight years.

Feeling Like Job

As I have stated earlier, my father passed in 2017, and my mother never got over my father's death. When Marla passed in 2018, I don't know if my mother really processed it very well. Her quality of life had diminished greatly after my dad died. That, plus the fact that she had a heart condition, which was operated on around the 2015 timeframe, that had returned to the original condition it was before the surgery. So she was reeling from both my father dying and her own physical ailments.

During this time, she could not offer me anything in the way of wisdom, comfort, or advice. I believe that I actually was able to offer her more in those areas than she was able to provide for me. Which I look back on and am very grateful to my God for allowing me to hopefully minister to my mother during the following year.

The new year of 2019 began unceremoniously. All of us went simply existing through the holidays. We got together and went through the motions, but that was really all there was during this season. I don't recall very much from this time. I do know that we didn't put a stitch of holiday decorations up at our house. We did travel to Greeneville, Tennessee, to spend time with my son Jordan, my mother, and my mother-in-law; but it was a very somber season and start to a new and very different year.

* * * * *

The year progressed mostly uneventful, or at least it felt that way. I did take another job during April of 2019 at the Savannah River Nuclear Site, which greatly reduced my responsibilities on the work front. I simply wanted to be away from the work that I had been doing to this point, no matter that I had taken a substantial reduction in salary. I just could not stomach the everyday interaction with people who placed importance upon things that had no real significance at all.

I could not continue with the facade of caring about things that were trivial in the grand scheme of life. I had learned a very painful lesson regarding what was truly important in life. No matter how hard you worked and climbed a career ladder, that ladder could be pulled out from under you at any given moment at no fault of your own.

Around June of 2019, my mother began to struggle in everyday living. This was due to her heart condition, which had reverted to the state it was in prior to having heart surgery in the 2015 timeframe. Much of this was not communicated to me during the time it was taking place, but I learned about much of what had happened after the fact.

Mom progressively became worse and, during the summer of 2019, was taken to the hospital emergency room on several occasions. She just could not really function in everyday life without becoming severely winded because her heart just wasn't capable of providing the blood flow she needed. There were times she would just collapse on the stairs or in the bathroom floor and lay there until she could muster the strength to get up. The majority of the time, she spent simply sitting in a recliner and watching TV or staring into space. I talked with Mom daily, as she made a point to call me every day just to hear my voice. I was able to visit many times and talk with her about spiritual topics.

During a week in the summer, she was moved briefly to a nursing home to try and regain strength just for everyday living. I remember going to see her during this time, and I could tell by the way she acted she could not stand being in this nursing home but knew that there was no other alternative. Even though, on numerous occasions, I had offered for her to move in with us in Augusta, she absolutely would not entertain the idea.

The very first week in October of 2019, right after the one-year anniversary of Marla passing, my mom was again taken to the emergency room from the nursing home. This time her condition deteriorated rapidly. I believe, at some point, she had given up on living, although she would not have admitted it. Yet again, the medical profession stated there was nothing more they could do and, right on cue, began to administer pain medication to keep her comfortable.

My mother was a very athletic woman and had won many awards in basketball during her high school days. She had always presented this tough I-can-handle-things attitude. But during this time in the hospital and the pain she was enduring with her heart, the toughness dissolved, as she struggled to withstand the pain.

At one point, however, she did begin to sing a gospel hymn while lying there in that hospital bed. On October 3, 2019, my mother passed and entered the gates of heaven, where I know she was greeted by my father and my wife. So for the third consecutive year in a row, I had to walk down this all-too-familiar path yet again.

Although my afflictions did not occur rapid fire, within one day I quickly identified with Job at this point in my life. The struggle with grief and suffering is as old as humanity itself. The primary theme of Job, which is widely considered the oldest book of the Bible, is loss and suffering. More specifically, how Job dealt with the utter destruction of all he had, including his health. Job's response to the events, as well as how his wife and three companions responded. Their accusations for why these misfortunes happened and what Job should be doing to rectify his standing with God.

But Job isn't the only book of the Bible which deals with suffering. As a matter of fact, the Bible is the foremost authority regarding the issue of suffering. I challenge you to find a book that so frequently and candidly asks why God permits evil and allows the righteous to suffer.

Just three chapters into Genesis, we are given the account of the fall of mankind. The sinful actions of Adam and Eve and the immediate mental grief that followed. Genesis 3:7 says, "At that moment their eyes were opened, and they suddenly felt shame at their nakedness. So they sewed fig leaves together to cover themselves." At the very moment, they ate of the fruit, the vulnerability that comes from being naked emerged.

And this is only the beginning; think about the suffering when Cain killed Abel; Joseph was in prison; the captivity of Israel; the widow, Ruth; David's adultery; and the treatment of the prophets, just to name a few. Then we have the entire Book of Lamentations which chronicles the suffering of the Jewish people because of their rebellion against God.

From my personal experience having been raised in a Christian home and in church my entire life, the church itself has done a very poor job of preparing Christians for suffering. When I was a teenager, capable of understanding deeper theological instruction, I do not remember having any discussions about the suffering component that was catalogued throughout the Bible. Much of my life was spent in a Free Will Baptist denomination where the bulk of the preaching was to accept Christ to avoid being sent to hell, the standard hellfire and-brimstone sermon. The teaching that took place was rudimentary at best and failed to equip me for the harsh realities of everyday life.

There is a failure in most churches to teach a biblical viewpoint of suffering. And I can tell you personally, it leaves you ill-equipped for the reality of this life. Most people do not give any thought about dealing with suffering until it is upon them. I thought I was very sympathetic to those that had suffered, but I, too, was caught completely unprepared. I was not taught the Christian life would be so difficult. That it would, at times, seem unfair compared to those who are prospering unbelievers.

This leaves believers, especially the young or new converts, very vulnerable to non-Christian worldviews, especially in this social media-driven world we now find ourselves. In my opinion, this is why many young believers today turn their back on their faith after attending college. They are unprepared to answer questions from competing worldviews because of a lack of teaching not only by the church but, more importantly, in the home. They also do not have any idea of how to respond to the ridicule they will face. I believe this is why the Christian faith, primarily those who stand up for their faith, are labeled as ignorant and uneducated.

The subject of suffering will be raised at some point in some required class. I was the first in my immediate family to attend college and deal with this issue. I was not equipped at all for the philosophy class that I was required to take. I could not have presented a valid argument as to why I believed the way I did, much less challenge the question of why suffering, grief, and evil exists.

Randy Alcorn puts it this way: "A faith that leaves us unprepared for suffering is a false faith that deserves to be lost." He goes on to say, "Genuine faith will be tested. False faith will be lost."[3] How many today, at least in this country, base their belief on God by the lack of afflictions? Especially with the advent of the prosperity theology within the United States. How many people have bought into this theology only to come face-to-face at some point with the exact opposite in suffering? Most likely the next response is to begin questioning why God let them down and, in the process, possibly abandon their faith because it didn't deliver what they were led to believe it would.

Jesus said in John 16:33, "I have told you these things so that in Me you may have peace. You will have suffering in this world. Be courageous! I have conquered the world." Does Jesus say that you might have some suffering, or possibly you might be in an uncomfortable situation? No, He says, "You will," meaning that it is a certainty. Or as He told His disciples in John 15:18–20, "If the world hates you, understand that it hated Me before it hated you. If you were of the world, the world would love you as its own. However, because you are not of the world, but I have chosen you out of it, the world hates you. Remember the word I spoke to you: 'A slave is not greater than his master.' If they persecuted Me, they will also persecute you."

3   Randy Alcorn, *If God Is Good* (New York City, New York: WaterBrook Multnomah, 2009), 12, 32, 37.

CHAPTER 3

My Grief and Suffering

Initial Grief

The very first obstacle that I had to overcome was sleeping in my own bed. For most of the time during this bout with cancer, Marla was able to sleep in our bed. The only extended time in which she did not was the last two, maybe three, weeks of the battle. During this time, the hospice had delivered an adjustable bed that was put in our living room. Some nights, I slept on the couch beside her bed, but most nights I carried her to our bed. However, for the first two weeks after Marla left, I would not sleep in our bed. I slept on the couch.

During this period, I was still employed with Westinghouse at the Vogtle Units 3 and 4 project. Returning to work was another hurdle to get over, primarily because Marla would see me off to work every morning we had been together. She was very adamant about getting out of bed with me and doing this each and every morning. Many times, she would get up even when she wasn't feeling the greatest or was sick.

Returning to work was a massively empty experience. I had the largest part of my inspiration as a man—that of being a provider—removed, and I had absolutely no desire to continue in the work that I was doing at that time. The individuals I worked with were supportive and understanding. Thinking back to this time period, I was given a lot of grace from my employer. But I was quite literally going through the motions and doing the bare minimum of what I had to do in my job. Desperately looking for another job daily, even to the point of getting my real estate license during this time, to get away from the daily responsibilities that went with my current occupation.

As one might imagine, each one of my sons dealt with this situation in their very own unique way. Each of our sons have very distinct personalities, as one might presume. However, interestingly enough, there are some striking similarities between them, and especially between sets. Ironically, the similarities are attached to their names by absolutely no design of ours.

The two whose names begin with J, Jordan and Jacob, have similar traits. As well as the two whose middle names begin with A, Andrew and Aron. Even though these sets have some similar traits, similar likes, and similar preferences when it comes to a vocation, they still had very distinct ways of processing their mother's passing.

Jordan took to social media to proclaim the love and respect he has for his mom. William Andrew alludes to the fact that during the timeframe when hospice was assigned and had Marla on so much pain medication, he lost his mother then and dealt with it way before she left. Jacob and Dallas Aron, as you may recall, were with me when we watched their mother via FaceTime leave this world for her eternal home. Both were sobbing their little hearts out, and I was helpless in the ability to do anything for them at the time. What could I do?

Jacob has always been the person who talks, analyzes things, and works them out via words. He and his mother would spend countless hours discussing issues, mostly spiritual topics. So he and I have spent lots of time simply talking about this event and discussing how to use it for the glory of God.

Dallas Aron, the youngest, is in many ways the most mature but also the most sheltered. He had an unbelievable composure about him when the memorial events were taking place. He even delivered one of the most inspiring speeches I have ever heard at his mother's memorial service that was held here in Augusta. He delivered it without a tear nor a crack in his voice. I was utterly amazed.

As time would pass and as things would arise that evoked memories of his mom, I would ask him how he felt. He would hardly ever talk about his feelings. However, a little over three years after the event, he finally opened up to me one day as we were eating lunch together that he felt as if he was putting too much pressure on himself to find a girlfriend. I asked why he felt this way, and he told me he was, in some ways, trying to fill the void left by his mother. This was the first time that he had talked to me about how he was feeling and how it was affecting him.

I had no idea the extent to which my sister-in-law Misty was suffering with grief. I was an only child, so I do not understand what it is to have a sibling. To a certain extent, I guess you might say that in this area I am somewhat selfish. Not because I am a selfish person, but it is a byproduct of the fact that I had no brothers or sisters. I had plenty of cousins who I view as my siblings, but it is not quite the same.

There were three siblings in the Shelton family: Marlin, Marla, and Misty. Because both of their parents worked, Marla spent many years as the "caretaker" of the household and specifically her little sister Misty. During most of our married life together, we spent countless days, special occasions, and holidays with Misty and her family. Misty also decided to homeschool when her children became school age after seeing the benefits with Marla and our sons.

Because of this, I was very aware that Misty was having an extremely difficult time. But we hadn't really talked much about it with one another. We hadn't really figured it out yet because it was her and Marla who would talk with each other every day, not me. So there was a period where we were both lost without the connection through Marla. But one day, which must have been on a Friday at the time because I was home, I heard Marla's iPhone chime.

Being only a few months since she went home, I had not done anything with her phone being connected, mainly due to the fact that a lot of the homeschool information was being sent to her phone and email address. I would check it from time to time until my information was distributed to those who needed it. The main way the homeschool group would communicate was through an app called

Marco Polo. This app lets you record a video message which can be viewed live while you are recording it by those who are in your sphere or can be viewed later by those recipients when they are available. Primarily, it allows for groups of people to communicate large messages which are too large or complex to send as a text message.

This day, it was a notification from Misty that she was sending a Marco message to Marla. I didn't watch the message live, as the app will notify the sender you are there, because I didn't want to interrupt what Misty was needing to do. But after letting some time pass, I watched her message. Misty was crying significantly and talking with Marla. She was telling her how lost she was and that she really needed and missed her. After watching her message to Marla on Marco, I talked with her about it. From that point forward, we became much closer in our relationship. Our relationship evolved into more of a brother and sister instead of an in-law relationship.

Not long after, Misty sent me an email that I want to share. She writes:

> "I get so caught up in my flesh of selfishness, I forget, sometimes, that it is not about me. I ask God what am I going to do without her. I leaned on her for everything. I almost picked up the phone yesterday to tell her I talked to someone. We had birthdays together. We had holidays together. We homeschooled together. We even prepared the same meals some nights. We would say, 'We are so not sisters! How did we do that?' Sometimes, we would even wear the same things. She has always been a huge part of my life. She was full of wisdom and grace. I want to share something I wrote one night when I stayed with her in the hospital in July.

"She Was There

"When I was born, she was there. As I grew up, she was there. When I got my driver's license, she was there. She took me and let me drive her car. When mom left, she was there to pick up the mom pieces. When I graduated, she was there. When I got my first 'real' job, she told me how proud she was of me. When I accepted Jesus, she was there. When I was baptized, she was there getting baptized too. When daddy died, she was there to make sure I was taken care of. When I got married, she was there beside me. When I became a Sunday School teacher, she was there beside me as my assistant. She told me she was a better leader as a follower. When my kids were born, she was there. When I worked, she was there to take care of my kids. When we started homeschooling, she was there. When we moved to Augusta, she was there with food and a hand to help and so, so, much more. When our family had the flu, while battling cancer, she managed to find the strength to make us chicken noodle soup. When I had questions about life, she was there. She was always there. Always. What am I going to do when she is not there anymore?' God has told me through all of this, 'Let Me be your best friend.' I love you, and I pray for all of you boys!"

As you might guess, when I read this, I completely broke down. I still, to this day, cannot read it without tearing up. One thing that struck me when Misty shared this with me was that I was not the only one who was suffering greatly. I knew that Misty and Marla were very close, but I had no idea of the absolute impact that Marla had on her younger sister. I was completely at a loss for words to describe the love that they shared. I knew of Marla's love for her sister because of having lived with her for a long time, but I didn't know the capacity of Misty's love for Marla.

Mary, Marla's mother, has walked through some rough days after her little girl stepped into her eternal reward also. Marla was very close to her mother even though there were some struggles in the relationship early on during Marla's late teens and early twenties. Mary and Marla's father, Marlin, had divorced not very long after I had met Marla.

Marla didn't agree with this at all and was very vocal about it. But even though she was very much against the divorce, she did not turn her back on either her father or her mother. Mary had always fiercely protected Marla, as I stated in Chapter 2. So when this happened, I believe Mary had some flashbacks to those days, but this time realized that no matter how hard she wanted to protect Marla, things were not in her control. They were in the hands of God.

This is another relationship that deepened dramatically after this event. I had always had a wonderful relationship with my mother-in-law, way better than some of the stories I had heard and the way these relationships are depicted in media. But during and after this, Mary became far closer and more precious to me than just a mother-in-law.

Trying to Understand

My entire life was forever changed, to the point it was unrecognizable, within the span of a few months. I felt like I was looking at someone else's life, not my own. I began to question what I did or failed to do that brought these events to pass. I began to question why things like this are allowed to happen to good people. For me, it was a loud resounding, *Why!?* Why was it Marla and not me who had to suffer with cancer? Why was I left and chosen to endure this hardship? Why did my sons have their mother taken from them? I was angry, I was distraught, I was confused, and I felt utterly alone.

Jesus said in the Gospel of John 16:32, "Look: An hour is coming, and has come, when each of you will be scattered to his own home, and will leave Me alone. Yet I am not alone, because the

Father is with me." Even though I knew this theological promise from God, there was a long period of time where I felt abandoned. I knew my sons, my sister-in-law, and mother-in-law were there for me and suffering the same as I was; but I still felt alone after the dust settled from Marla's memorial services even to the point of being abandoned by my God.

I can honestly say that I did not question my faith in God, but I questioned why it felt as if he had abandoned me and had not answered our prayers. As C. S. Lewis stated in dealing with his grief over the loss of his wife to cancer, "Not that I am (I think) in much danger of ceasing to believe in God. The real danger is of coming to believe such dreadful things about Him."[4]

There were some very close and dear friends who were going out of their way to stay in touch during the first year or so after September 2018. However, ultimately the interactions became less over time, and the contact fell back to how it was before these events happened or they ceased altogether. This kind of reminded me of when Peter said to Jesus that he would never abandon Jesus and would even die for him, and then denied Christ three times before the cock crowed.

I wept bitterly on many occasions, sometimes screaming at the top of my lungs. Even though I was acting like a spoiled child who doesn't get their way by shouting, yelling, screaming, and crying to God for answers. He began, very patiently, speaking to me through various mediums.

As I said earlier, I was unprepared for suffering and was mostly in denial. So I began searching for answers. I consumed anything I could find on grieving. I read books and listened to many discussions on the topic. Obviously, I was looking for Christian resources. I attended a dealing-with-grief group at my church. With all of these elements designed to help me navigate the uncharted waters, the most insight I gained came primarily from the first book I read which was not even about grief. But I believe the message shared with

---

[4]   C. S. Lewis, *A Grief Observed* (New York City, New York: HarperCollins, 1996), 6, 18, 49.

me through this book was delivered directly by the Maker Himself. Wisdom and peace that surpasses all human understanding, as Scripture testifies.

One day, shortly after the memorial services for Marla had ended, I was sitting on the couch, and a book that had been sitting on the coffee table grabbed my attention. It had set there for many months and had literally become part of the decor, but this particular day, it seemed to jump off the table and into my hands, begging for me to read it. The book was written by Randy Alcorn and is entitled, *If God Is Good: Faith in the Midst of Suffering and Evil.* I believe that Misty, my sister-in-law, had purchased this book for Marla during her battle with cancer.

To my knowledge, Marla never opened the book, and there it sat on the coffee table for months and months. What later amazed me was that I realized that God did not intend for this book to be read by Marla but knew that I was the one who would need to read it when the time came. I picked up the book and began to read and could not put it down. God began speaking to me through this book in ways as if He were personally reading or telling me the insights himself. God's voice, through the Holy Spirit, spoke so clearly to me that it might as well have been audible and possibly might have been in that still small voice with which He speaks.

Now you might be looking at the subtitle of the book, *Faith in the Midst of Suffering and Evil*, and be thinking to yourself, *Isn't suffering different that grief?* Meaning that one usually associates suffering as being a physical form of pain or is the direct result of the actions of another individual beyond the control of the victim. *Suffering* is defined as "the bearing of pain or distress," while *grief* is defined as "the source or cause of deep mental anguish." So while these terms seem to denote a slight difference with each other, they are in fact synonymous, almost identical. Both refer to extreme or severe pain, with anguish adding that it can be both mental and physical.

I was bearing the distress of deep mental anguish because my lovely wife was afflicted and suffered with a disease which ultimately took her life at the young age of forty-five and only twenty-three years into our marriage. Or to further break these terms down to their root, one could simply say I was in extreme mental pain. So for me, suffering and grieving were identical, one and the same.

But as I began to read this book, I, too, tended to lean in my thinking that suffering was more a physical manifestation. My wife having to suffer the pain of cancer. Not until I was much further into the book did I start to realize that I was mentally suffering. I certainly knew I was grieving tremendously, but I didn't realize that part of that process was suffering the pain of being separated from the one I loved, suffering from regret for things I failed to do, and suffering the guilt of wanting to trade places with her.

Not only was this suffering manifesting itself in my mental state but it was impacting me physically as well. I didn't completely let everything get to me to the point that I sat down and wallowed in my situation. Although at times that's all I felt like doing. Quite the contrary, for me, the most therapeutic state was to be as busy as I could be. So I still managed to somehow exercise as I had always done since I was a young. Subliminally, I suppose it became a coping mechanism, although I wasn't thinking of it in that way, nor was I using exercise to alleviate the pain and associated stress that results. I also immersed myself in home-improvement projects every weekend, busily working to upgrade something around the house, just as we had discussed before the cancer.

I don't recall in any of the resources, videos, and group meetings there being any discussion about the suffering component of grief. Or at least discussing the fact that these emotional states are actually one and the same. It was just grief and grieving, as if it were some special type of category unto itself designated for people who are going through certain life-changing events. There was very little, if any, mention of the "suffering that you must be feeling."

Why do I point out what might possibly be, to many, the obvious? I believe human beings throughout history, but especially in today's society, tend to rank everything in some manner, whether it be in terms of pleasure, difficulty, severity, or intensity. So suffering would then seemingly rank higher in terms of intensity than grief even though they are, in fact, identical states. Add to this the concept that every person experiences some form of grief on a daily basis but are unaware they are actually experiencing it.

Granger E. Westberg writes:

> If we include our "little griefs" along with our "large griefs," we can say that grief is as natural to every person as breathing. It is inevitable! You cannot live without experiencing it in a thousand different ways. Such a seemingly inconsequential thing as your husband's phoning at the last minute, just before guests are arriving for dinner, to say that he has to work late throws you into a mild form of grief. Or perhaps the boss under, whom you have worked happily for ten years, is suddenly transferred, and the new one is pompous and overbearing. This is a form of grief. How you handle these "little griefs" will, in some measure, tell you how you will handle the larger griefs when they come.[5]

Adding this into the comparison would then lead to an even further categorization. One would then rank the forms of grief itself. Meaning, the "larger griefs," as Mr. Westberg defined, would rank higher in severity than those of the everyday "little" variety.

I realized very quickly that the vast majority of people are quite uneasy and do not know what to do or what to say to someone who is in the middle of suffering (large griefs) due to what life has thrown their way, especially for someone who must endure multiple events in a short period of time.

From my experience over the course of three consecutive years and laying three of the closest people in my life to rest, most will compartmentalize the two emotions and do not associate suffering with grieving. For that matter, most people do not even realize they

---

[5] Granger E. Westberg, *Good Grief* (Minneapolis City, Minneapolis: Fortress Press, 1971), 13.

grieve on a daily basis. I believe primarily it is a product of misinterpretation of those "little griefs" which happen daily and are not to be counted as suffering when they occur. They are simply viewed as merely the issues of everyday life. So when these large griefs occur, which conveys a great deal of mental suffering, most people are caught off guard.

Friends of those who are walking the path seem quite uncomfortable to spend too much time around those that are grieving. Most likely these people abhor the thoughts of what it would be like if they were to trade places and quickly dismiss any thoughts as to how they would handle the situation. They don't want to think about it, as it is a very painful reminder to people that at any given moment, it could be them who is standing in that place, so they are very quick distance themselves from these situations.

C. S. Lewis also recognized this: "If I had really cared, as I thought I did, about the sorrows of the world, I should not have been so overwhelmed when my own sorrow came."[6] I remember thinking about this quite extensively very early in my process of grieving. And I realized that no matter how empathic you believe yourself to be, you cannot really understand or imagine the suffering that comes with those "larger griefs" when they visit you.

And visit you they will, as Jesus said in John 16:33. The primary reason I felt led to write this book is to try and prepare anyone who reads it for the suffering which is to come. To hopefully offer some spiritual strength to someone who may be suffering at this very moment.

As I said earlier, most people do not give any thought whatsoever to suffering, myself included. I thought I had an idea, but I had no idea until I was right in the middle of it. I was then in no position to deal with it in the least bit. I felt forced to find a way to process the suffering all the while I was dazed, exhausted, and pressed to get the things done that need immediate attention. It was actually quite

---

[6]   C. S. Lewis, *A Grief Observed* (New York City, New York: HarperCollins, 1996), 6, 18, 49.

infuriating that I could not just sit down and mentally try to cope what had just happened.

I was able to handle the passing of my father mainly, I believe, because I was able to think through the sorrow well in advance. Having been involved in sports from an early age, one thing that I remember being coached on was to envision yourself competing well. If you visualize in your mind being successful on the playing field, then that will greatly enhance your chances of achieving that success. As a child, you know that—barring some catastrophic event—you will deal with the death of your parents someday. And once they reach a certain age and begin having more health issues that need attention, these thoughts move to the forefront of your mind. I remember I would think through the steps that would take place once they passed.

I realize this sounds somewhat morbid, and I don't mean that I thought about it very often—actually only on a couple occasions. But I believe this helped prepare me for the grieving that was to follow when it did occur. Now having said this, there was not a moment in which I thought of, for the briefest of seconds, the passing of my beloved wife. As a matter of fact, being three years older than she, I fully expected that I would be the one to depart first. Up to the point the appendicitis began, neither of us had any physical ailments to speak of. She had dealt with a goiter in the mid-2000s, but other than that, neither of us went for anything more than a physical checkup. The thought never darkened my mind as to what I would do without her.

In the foreword to *A Grief Observed* by C. S. Lewis, Madeleine L'Engle writes, "The death of a beloved is an amputation. But when two people marry, each one has to accept that one of them will die before the other."[7] Her statement is predicated upon a "long and fulfilling marriage." One must then define the time period which constitutes "long." Marla and I were married twenty-three years, and due to the staggering divorce rate in the United States, that would

7 C. S. Lewis, *A Grief Observed* (New York City, New York: HarperCollins, 1996), 6, 18, 49.

probably be considered a long marriage in today's terms. But when neither of us had yet turned fifty years old, nor had the opportunity to celebrate the first of the momentous anniversaries, the twenty-fifth, then I don't think it was a very long marriage at all.

Only on the briefest of occasions did a glimpse of thought run through my brain about one dying before the other. And as I said earlier, it was me who typically would be first due to age and gender, so the brief thought was in relation to who would take care of Marla. In that we have four sons, the answer was quite obvious, and therefore no further energy was expended on that unpleasant thought.

You may be asking yourself, *Okay, Dallas what's your point? Do I need to spend an inordinate amount of time on the dark thoughts of my spouse dying? Or should I begin some subconscious form of distancing myself from my spouse, a mental bracing of oneself for the inevitable that is to come?* I am absolutely not insinuating either of the two, especially the latter.

What I am saying, as cliché' as it will sound, is to love your mate to the absolute best of your ability no matter what your age. To live with the intention of uplifting one another each day in whatever form that takes. To speak each other's love language and keep their love tank topped off or running over. To not squander one single second of the precious time God has granted each of us on this planet.

In the end, the problems of this life are trivial. The daily "little griefs" that abound are mere inconveniences compared to when the time comes, and you no longer can enjoy the pleasure of their companionship. I have heard so often, as I am sure you have as well, that no one says at the end of their life that they wished they would have spent more time at the office, or climbed higher on the corporate ladder, etc. No, almost always it is something to the effect of, "I wish I would have spent more time with my spouse viewing the sunset or took my kids to more special places."

I came face-to-face with the staggering realization of the brevity of this life at what I would consider the young age of forty-eight. James 4:14 says, "You don't even know what tomorrow will bring— what your life will be! For you are like smoke that appears for a little while, then vanishes." My father would always tell me how fast time went, but after having lived through these events, I began to understand quite well the significance of this verse and what my dad was trying to tell me.

Time is indeed very short, and no one knows what will happen a few minutes from now—least of all in the next year. I feel it is imperative as believers that we realize just how brief our time here on earth is. So that we can try and really grasp the fact that we are just passing through this life. That there is something unbelievably better for those who have placed their faith in Jesus Christ.

One thing that has become crystal clear to me after living through the last two years of this pandemic is, there are an enormous part of the United States population who are intensely afraid of death. Even worse, I firmly believe there are large masses of people, especially Christians, who believe they are guaranteed to live to a ripe old age. But this is not the case; nowhere are we guaranteed the very next breath we take.

Let's revisit the parable of the rich fool recorded in Luke 12:13–21. Recall this was the rich man whose land was very productive. He then began to think to himself, *What am I going to do with all these crops?* He then decided that he would tear down his barns and build bigger ones to store his immense bounty. Were these actions sinful and wrong? I don't think they were because we are directed to be good stewards of what God has blessed us with.

The problem became when he thought to himself that his goods would last him for many years. That he would then retire, take it easy, eat, drink, and enjoy himself. Sounds quite familiar, does it not? Again, why was this wrong? Because he had placed his faith in his wealth and not God, who incidentally provided him with his wealth. Was his wealth able to save him from the events that were about to take place? Jesus said in Luke 12:21, "That's how it is with the one who stores up treasure for himself and is not rich toward God."

Most of us live daily as if tomorrow is a certainty. We go throughout the weeks and months looking ahead to the future. Not one of us knows when they will hear God say to them, *This very night, your life is demanded of you.*

CHAPTER 4

Resilient Believers, Suffering, and Grieving

Responses to Suffering

I would venture to assume that many in the ancient world viewed suffering as a result of angering a deity. Job was accused by his friends of sinning against God. Moreover, they implored him to repent of sinning even though Job explained that he had not sinned. In essence, Job's friends were saying, "You had to have sinned, or else God would not be imposing judgement against you." And we know from the first chapter that Job had done nothing wrong but was being accused of being faithful to God because of his good lifestyle. How many people, especially in the United States, are faithful as long as things are going well?

But there are also those throughout history who have pondered the suffering of humankind as a means to question if God cares about us, or if He exists because there is suffering. Many an atheist has used the evil and suffering of the world as an answer to the question of God's existence. Three centuries before Christ, the Greek philosopher Epicurus held that the gods exist but have absolutely no concern for, or even awareness of, humankind. Indeed, for the gods to involve themselves in the menial matters of men would be to perturb the supreme happiness and tranquility that characterizes and defines them.[8]

Modern atheists are no different; they continue to use the premise that because of the suffering and evil is rampant in the world, God cannot exist. In their view, God is neither omnipotent nor all-loving because He allows suffering to exist. David Hume posed these questions about God. "Why is there any misery at all in the world? Not by chance surely. For some cause then. Is it from the intention of the deity? But He is perfectly benevolent. Is it contrary to his intentions? But He is almighty. Nothing can shake the solidity of this reasoning, so short, so clear, so decisive."[9] The conclusion that Mr. Hume is driving at is either God is not all-loving by allowing suffering, or God is not all-powerful to stop the world's suffering.

One of the more preeminent atheists of this generation, Richard Dawkins, states in his book, *The God Delusion,* that it is as easy to imagine an evil God as a good one. In fact, he considers the God of the Old Testament an evil deity.[10]

C. S. Lewis, who was an atheist who came to Christ, wrote, "Not many years ago when I was an atheist, if anyone had asked me, 'Why do you not believe in God?,' my reply would have run something like this: 'Look at the universe we live in... History is largely a record of crime, war, disease, and terror... But all civilizations pass away and, even while they remain, inflict peculiar sufferings of their own... Every race that comes into being in any part of the universe is doomed; for the universe, they tell us, is running down... All stories will come to nothing: all life will turn out in the end to have been a transitory and senseless contortion upon the idiotic face of infinite matter. If you ask me to believe that this is the work of a benevolent and omnipotent spirit, I reply that all the evidence points in the

8 Neel Burton, *The Philosophy of Epicurus* (2019), https://www.psychologytoday.com.
9 David Hume, *Dialogues Concerning Natural Religion* (London: William Blackwood, 1907), 134, 140.
10 Randy Alcorn, *If God Is Good* (New York City, New York: WaterBrook Multnomah, 2009), 12, 32, 37.

opposite direction. Either there is no spirit behind the universe, or else a spirit indifferent to good and evil, or else an evil spirit.'"[11]

Think for a moment: if God were to be true to these assessments, what would have taken place after Adam and Eve disobeyed his command? The human race would have ended before it began.

If we hold the view that God is malevolent rather than benevolent, then God would have had a couple of options in dealing with this insubordination. He could have ended the lives of Adam and Eve right on the spot for disobeying him. He would also have had the option of removing the capability of producing any children, thus again ending the human race from perpetuating. Either of these options would have eliminated the suffering which was to be extended to all humanity because of their original sin and the curse placed upon the earth.

However, would these have been the more loving and gracious acts? The No Tolerance policy that we as humans are so quick to evoke, especially in this era of a "virtue-signaling" society. After all, God gave them a warning in Genesis 2:17, "But you must not eat from the tree of the knowledge of good and evil, for on the day you eat from it, you will certainly die." What if that warning had indeed been literal? In essence, God warned them that you yourself won't immediately die, but you will suffer in life, your life will end, and all those who come after you will suffer from the curse that you have caused.

This was the first recorded use of the pride of life trap. One that Satan has used ever since, and one that we all fall victim to at some point in our lives. The pride-of-life deception that told Eve she would be like God: knowing good and evil. That God was withholding this wisdom from them. The same pride-of-life deception that says an all-loving God should not allow suffering to exist in the world. The same suffering that exists because humans continue to fall for the lie over and over, creating more and more suffering upon one another.

---

[11] C. S. Lewis, *The Problem of Pain* (New York City, New York: Macmillan, 1962), 13–15.

Are you seeing the pattern? Do you see the individual ultimately responsible for suffering? Satan said, "No, you will not die," and snickers when we proceed to point our finger at God and ask, "Why don't you stop this, God? Why didn't you warn us? Why don't you save us?"

To which God replies, "I did warn you, but I also made a way for you to make amends."

I was no different when Marla died. I fell for the old deception that as a Christian, I was supposed to be protected from tragedies such as this. Like so many Christians, especially here in this privileged nation, I felt as if I had somehow earned status with God because I was his child. My Christian insurance policy against disaster and calamity. Randy Alcorn states, "Sufferers have told me, 'We did everything right. We attended church and gave our money to missions—and then God did this to us. I don't get it.'"[12]

There is no place that I can find in the Bible that God has assured us that if we believe in Him and make good decisions based upon His will, we will be spared from suffering. Actually, quite the contrary is described in many places throughout both the Old and New Testaments. Take for instance the story of Meshach, Shadrach, and Abednego. Their decision to follow God above all else resulted in a death penalty. Granted there was a miraculous, God-exalting rescue. But their choice still resulted in what was intended to be a very painful immediate death.

Then there is the life story of Paul. This man was a prominent pharisee within the Jewish community. He had a pure-blooded Jewish lineage, was highly educated, and held a position of authority. Then he decided, after his encounter with Jesus, that he would submit to Jesus and give all those things up. His godly calling and decision resulted in numerous beatings, jail sentences, and even shipwrecks where he came close to dying.

I didn't get it either. But as the thoughts were going through my mind that we did things as best as we could, God reminded me that

---

[12] Randy Alcorn, *If God Is Good* (New York City, New York: WaterBrook Multnomah, 2009), 12, 32, 37.

He did not promise His children would gain some sort of immunity from the evils, pains, and suffering of this world. Paraphrasing what Jesus said in John 15:20 and 16:33, "They persecuted me, what do you think they will do to you? You will suffer in this world, but be courageous (be of good cheer) because I have conquered the world."

Do you understand why it is important to be able to offer a response to suffering? Because there are many people who will gravitate to the conclusion that if there is an all-loving God, then human suffering should not occur. Therefore, maybe an all-loving God does not exist. Or worse, for a believer who has placed their faith in God but has not endured suffering may quickly lose their faith, or realize their faith in God was really based upon their continued prosperity. Faith based upon something other than God and God alone needs to be lost. As has been said previously, suffering is not if but when.

There are many other worldview variations relating to why suffering and evil exist. But I believe the explanation given in the Bible is the greatest and most reassuring: to understand that God absolutely abhors evil but is able to use it for good. And above all else, that one day God will eliminate evil and suffering altogether gives me a far greater hope.

Encouragement that someday, there will no longer be suffering as Revelation 21:4, "He will wipe away every tear from their eyes. Death will no longer exist, grief, crying, and pain will exist no longer, because the previous things have passed away." No matter to what degree or to what extent, everyone experiences pain, grief, and suffering in this sin-cursed world. But Christians have that to look forward to even in the midst of the pain.

So I ask you: do you need to adjust your perspective? Do you need to get rid of a false sense of security due to your faith and your blessings? Or are you prepared for the day when things turn upside down and the pain becomes unbearable?

Insights from Job

Growing up in a small rural county in East Tennessee, I remembered hearing the older people make remarks about the patience of

Job. Most likely because I had no patience at all when I was young, I still don't have much. But I am not sure where that was derived from the Book of Job. I am not quite sure the connection between patience and the suffering described in Job.

Yes, at the end of the first chapter—when Job had lost all his possessions and his children—it is recorded in Job 1:20–21, "He fell to the ground and worshipped, saying 'Naked I came from my mother's womb, and naked I will leave this life. The Lord gives, and the Lord takes away. Praise the name of Yahweh.'"

At the end of Chapter 2, after Job's health was taken from him and his own wife had told him to "curse God and die!," Job 2:10 says, "'You speak as a foolish woman speaks,' he told her. 'Should we accept only good from God and not adversity?' Throughout all this, Job did not sin in what he said."

But in the very next chapter, we see that Job's mental state quickly went downhill. The weight of what has just occurred may have finally set in because Job 3:1 reads, "After this, Job began to speak and cursed the day he was born." He then goes on a lengthy tirade, wishing the day he was born did not take place. He even questions, in verse 11, "Why was I not stillborn?"

Finally at the end of Chapter 3, Job concludes by saying these words. Job 3:20–22 states, "Why is light given to one burdened with grief, whose existence is bitter, who wait for death, but it does not come, and search for it more than for hidden treasure, who are filled with much joy and are glad when they reach the grave?" Where in the world did we get that Job was a supernatural model of patience? Now we don't know the exact timeframe of the events recorded; however, I suspect that very little time had passed from when Job's health was stricken to when he lamented even being born in Chapter 3.

I know this was exactly the case with my ordeal. I was walking around in a dazed-and-confused state for many months, not really feeling what had just happened. Until suddenly one day the flood gates opened, and I could not contain my sorrow. It was on that day that I called Mary, my mother-in-law, sobbing and apologizing that it was my fault that Marla had died. I don't remember the date, day, or time; but I remember I was walking down the road toward the local middle school when it happened, and I could not get a hold of myself. I suspect this may have been the case with Job when Chapter 3 begins.

Job is an extremely insightful book that gets very little attention. There are profound—and yes, difficult—lessons that Job offers on suffering. Not only on how to navigate through suffering well but also on what not to say to fellow believers who are in the midst of severe suffering.

First let's think about who is really responsible for human suffering. The first two chapters of Job offer great insight into this question. We read that God is very pleased with His righteous servant Job, but it is Satan who comes in to accuse Job of only worshipping God because of the great benefits he receives from God. Job 1:9–10 reads, "Satan answered the Lord, 'Does Job fear God for nothing? Haven't You placed a hedge around him, his household, and everything he owns? You have blessed the work of his hands, and his possessions have increased in the land.'"

We read this verse, but do we really think about what it tells us about God's normal policy for His servants? The second fact that I believe this verse also tells us is what we can expect if we are someone of "perfect integrity," as God described Job.

I believe these verses tell us that God's normal plan for His servants is one of both spiritual and earthly blessings. Job had what one would call a picture-perfect life. How do I know that? Because we know from a biblical standpoint that the number seven indicates perfection.

Job had seven sons and three daughters, and in verse 4, we read that the sons take turns in having banquets at their homes and inviting their sisters to join them. So not only did Job have a large family but there is also an indication that it was a happy household. The children are consistently initiating family reunions and including their sisters. Not only a happy family life but Job was also very wealthy, and verse 3 tells us Job was the "greatest man among all the people of the east." This indicates that he was also a man of prominence. Job appears to have had it all.

However, I find it interesting that the only person spared was Job's wife. Why was that? The only mention of Job's wife is Job 2:9 where she tells Job that he should just curse God and die. We are not told, but it appears that she was left unharmed because she actually added to the anguish that Satan was inflicting upon Job. She did the exact thing Satan claimed Job would do once all his blessings were taken away.

Although this is the only time she spoke, she may have delivered more torment in this one brief statement than Job's friends did in all of their speeches combined. This was the one person who should have been Job's biggest and most loving supporter. Yet she was the first one who told him that he should give up and die. Can you imagine those words coming from your spouse during this type of ordeal? The person who should love you more than anyone else on Earth basically tells you that you should just get it over with.

Next these verses tell believers what to anticipate from the accuser, Satan. Satan accuses Job of worshipping God for the benefits he receives in doing so. I find it interesting that Satan focused on the fear aspect of Job's relationship with the almighty Creator of the Universe. Satan asks, "Does Job fear God for nothing?" To me this indicates that Satan is blaming Job of only worshipping out of fear of losing his possessions and his status.

I believe this is crucial key point of the Book of Job. One that is very easily overlooked or maybe not even recognized at all. Satan goes on to make a second accusation in verse 11, saying in essence, "take everything he owns away, and Job will curse you to your face." To curse God to his face would be the ultimate transgression, a direct confrontation and utter rejection of God himself.

I believe this is an essential reason that God allowed Job to suffer. To demonstrate not only to Satan but to Job himself that God's servants simply love Him for who He is, irrespective of the temporal earthly blessings that may come along with a relationship with Him. God may then allow a drastic change in plan toward His children in order to prove the authenticity and sincerity of our relationship with Him—although we may not see it at first, and we definitely do not enjoy having to endure these setbacks.

Additionally, this first chapter of Job shows believers that the more they are in line with God's will, the bigger of a target to Satan you will become. The greater of a threat you become to the enemy, the more the enemy wants to take you down and leave you devastated. I am sure there were other God-fearing men during Job's time, such as his so-called friends, but Job was making a profound impact upon his community, as we see later in the book.

Out of these two points comes a few questions I want you to consider. The first question is, Would God boast about your integrity and relationship with Him? Do you love God for God, or are you more in love with what He has blessed you with? Finally, are you prepared for the attacks that are sure to come your way?

Many people believe that God is ultimately responsible for human suffering because He can prevent the suffering that we endure. And as we see in the first chapter of Job, this is an accurate belief, as hard as it may be to grasp. However, let's not forget that God was not the one to inflict these sufferings upon Job: Satan was the one who initiated the events that produced these tragedies. But yes, the hard part for all of us to swallow is that God conceded control over Job's life to the Accuser.

Douglas Sean O'Donnell writes, "What is surprising is his theology. Is God in the business of dealing with Satan? Or worse, is God in the business of giving authority to Satan? Worse still, Is God in the business of giving Satan power to do evil to good people? The answer to those questions is yes. But the key to understanding why yes is the right answer is to understand and rightly apply the final phrase from our final verse, namely, 'So Satan went out from the presence of the Lord' (Job 12). This ending leaves little doubt concerning who is in control of Satan, the world, and even what is soon to befall one person living at one time in one obscure place in the world."[13]

With this in mind, next we need to look briefly at the different reasons God allows His children to suffer. The most obvious, and the easiest to understand, is the penalty of sin. The suffering one endures

---

[13] Douglas Sean O'Donnell, "Why Was Satan Allowed to Torment Job? (Job 1)," (2020), https://www.crossway.org/articles.

physically for a disease they may have contracted by engaging in some illicit act. "Biblically, sin always leads to suffering, and the suffering always outweighs whatever fleeting pleasure the sin gives."[14]

The concept of retribution is so engrained in us as a human race we tend to view everything through the lens of reaping what you sow. After all, that is a biblical principal, right? Scripture, both the Old and New Testaments, affirms this concept. The exile of the Israelites after they continued to worship false gods, the punishment of David for his sin with Bathsheba, and the immediate death of Ananias and Sapphira all attest to the consequences of sin.

The next, almost as easily recognizable purpose, is for spiritual growth. God uses suffering to provide His child with valuable insight that would not have been obtained by any other means. In the New Testament, both Paul and James speak of the endurance that afflictions produce. Paul writes in Romans 5:3 and 4, "And not only that but we also rejoice in our afflictions, because we know that affliction produces endurance, endurance produces proven character, and proven character produces hope."

The Book of James, which happens to be my personal favorite, records in James 1:2–4, "Consider it a great joy, my brothers, whenever you experience various trials, knowing that the testing of your faith produces endurance. But endurance must do its complete work, so that you may be mature and complete, lacking nothing."

The next purpose for suffering is one that, in my opinion, is almost identical to spiritual growth, and that is for the glorification of Jesus Christ. To exalt the one and only Savior of the human race in the hopes of drawing others to Him. I believe, for those of us who have lived since Jesus lived, that these two outcomes tend to go hand in hand. We as believers are being sanctified each day, or at least we should be moving toward that goal. We learn and grow, while at the same time, in that growth, we glorify the one and only risen Christ.

We can see this in the recording of when Jesus's disciples asked of Him, What sin did the blind man commit to cause him to be

---

[14] Eric Ortlund, *Suffering Wisely and Well: The Grief of Job and the Grace of God* (Wheaton, Illinois: Crossway, 2022), 17, 73, 128.

blind? John 9:1–5, "As He was passing by, He saw a man blind from birth. His disciples questioned Him: 'Rabbi, who sinned, this man or his parents, that he was born blind?' 'Neither this man nor his parents sinned,' Jesus answered. 'This came about so that God's works might be displayed in him.'" This blind man and, most likely his parents as well, had a life's worth of suffering to be used by Jesus Himself not only so that He would be exalted but also to grow the disciples spiritually. We are not told much of the blind man's reaction to this event, nor the impact this made upon him spiritually. But one would think that blind man walked away from his encounter with Jesus with far greater spiritual insight of Jesus than before.

Another example is the history of the early church recorded in Acts. The apostles and early believers experienced some of the greatest persecutions in the history of the world. Each one of the apostles was executed for His faith and refusal to renounce that Jesus is the Messiah. The Roman Emperor Nero accused Christians for the Great Fire of Rome in AD 64 mainly to divert attention, as some suspected Nero of starting the fire himself.

The result of this was a large number of Christians being put to death in the most horrific manner possible. These believers were crucified; sown up in animal skins so dogs could rip them apart; and even covered in pitch, nailed to posts, and burned as torches to light up the night. Although not as horrific, but equally as cruel, these persecutions would continue for well over two hundred years.

It wasn't until AD 311 the Roman rulers essentially were exhausted in carrying out all the executions. What ended up being the result of this intense suffering? It strengthened and emboldened other believers to remain firm or to even become more aggressive in sharing of the Gospel of Christ. As was mentioned earlier, it ultimately removed those with false faith.

This brings me to the last purpose of how God uses suffering I would like to discuss: the one on full display in the Book of Job and the one that is the hardest for believers to understand and accept. This purpose is to bring the believer to the place where we desire and value our relationship with God. Where God is loved and honored simply because He is God. In other words, we love God for God alone and for no other reason. How else are we to be happy spending eternity with Him? This is what we see taking place in Job, and it is the purpose that God allows believers to go through ordeals similar to Job.

This is the fork in the road where the all-sufficiency of God really goes from the theoretical to the practical. It absolutely was for me even though I had not the faintest idea about this particular form of spiritual purpose before being thrust into the middle of it. And just as Job struggled with why these things were befalling him, I, too, struggled tremendously.

I believe this is the primary way in which God works to prepare our souls for an eternity with Him. I also firmly believe that Jesus Himself alluded to this when He said in Luke 14:26, "If anyone comes to me and does not hate his own father and mother, wife, and children, brothers, and sisters—yes, and even his own life—he cannot be my disciple." This is another passage that is very hard for believers to understand. But it seems to me that Jesus was saying that "to be my disciple, you must love me for me alone." All earthly relationships in your life will appear to others as if they are despised in comparison with your relationship to Christ.

God sometimes uses these Job-like torments not because He is angry with us or wanting to teach us some deep spiritual lesson but to demonstrate to us the reality that we cannot survive in this life apart from a relationship with Him. The point where the rubber meets the road of our faith. The place where all the righteous and spiritual actions we thought were producing in us this "highly spiritual, godly, sanctified person" gets thrust into the purifying fire of reality. How we perceived our spiritual condition gets tested beyond anything we imagined. What will remain after you have been tested by this fire?

Many today have a skewed view of God based upon the influence of the current culture, which is ever changing and shifting. This is why a biblical worldview is needed now more than ever in the culture we live in. Randy Alcorn writes, "This entertainment-driven and self-gratification-obsessed blend of pop psychology, pop philosophy, and pop theology has become its own worldview. Never have people needed to hear the biblical worldview more—and perhaps never have they been more culturally conditioned to dismiss it."[15]

Unfortunately, twisted worldviews have affected Christians as well. Many believers do not have a solid biblical base from which to draw strength from. Others may have once had a strong base knowledge only to have let the numerous distractions of modern society choke out the time they spend in the Word. Still there are others who stay away from the "uncomfortable" parts of the Bible. The hard-to-understand parts, or those that don't produce the positive emotions. Even many pastors or leaders of churches spend very little, if any, time on these parts of Scripture.

There is such a disproportionate amount of time spent on the positive parts of the Bible, such as Jeremiah 29:11, "For I know the plans I have for you"—this is the Lord's declaration— "plans for your welfare, not for disaster, to give you a future and a hope." I have seen this piece of scripture used so often for almost every occasion, which is grief-producing—whether small or large.

But what I find interesting is the remainder of the passage of Chapter 29 is left out. This was a letter that Jeremiah sent to those who had been deported to Babylon. And the most interesting thing is verse 10, right before verse 11, which says, "For this is what the Lord says: 'When seventy years for Babylon are complete, I will attend to you and will confirm My promise concerning you to restore you to this place.'"

Do you think the older Israelites found this message uplifting? I kind of doubt it. This was an overall message to the nation of Israel, but to those who were going to die in captivity, I really doubt—for them, personally—they were thinking good things about the message being delivered. Honestly, this may not have been a positive message for any of them at that time. I would think that being told you were about to spend the next seventy years in captivity would not produce a very positive outlook.

---

[15] Randy Alcorn, *If God Is Good* (New York City, New York: WaterBrook Multnomah, 2009), 12, 32, 37.

Think this through for a moment: the captivity of the Jews by Babylon was punishment for their disobedience to God. Those who were faithful were enduring the same punishment as those who were unfaithful and being given the message that "After seventy years, I will restore you to this place." Do you think that the faithful ones found this message encouraging? Do you think they were questioning why they were suffering for remaining faithful?

This is why the soundbite generation that has evolved over the past several years is struggling with their worldview, even those who are Christians. And the churches have not only fallen into the same snare but, in many cases, have led people into this situation. I am thinking of the emphasis on the catchy slogans put on church signs, or the immersion into social media some churches have embraced. The emphasis placed on these positive verses being used for any given situation have lured Christians into thinking that nothing devastating should happen to them in this life. And the Bible affirms that this is simply not true.

I believe this is also a part of what Jesus Himself said in Matthew 7:13–14, "Enter through the narrow gate. For the gate is wide and the road is broad that leads to destruction, and there are many who go through it. How narrow is the gate and difficult the road that leads to life, and few find it." I do not know of a single person, believer or not, who would choose the harder road in life. But here Jesus is saying that to enter the kingdom, the road is going to be difficult.

One other translation of the word used here for difficult is "press hard upon." I believe another point being made by Jesus in this verse is, be certain of which gate you have chosen. Because life will be difficult for those who choose the narrow gate that leads to the kingdom. And if you believe only good things are to happen to you once you become a Christian, then maybe you have mistakenly chosen the wide gate instead, and you will, at some point, come to the place where you will have a course correction. A fork in the road where the narrow path keeps getting even more narrow, and you realize that God is all you needed and all you ever want. Or the seemingly narrow path you were on opens up to a broader path where you question why God allowed this cruel thing to happen to you, and you subsequently turn away from the only source of life itself.

How Not to Comfort Those Suffering

I have had some opportunities arise where someone I know has said to me they don't know what to say to someone who is suffering. Having been on the receiving end of those conversations, I know the things I didn't want to hear at the time. This is an equally as vital lesson from the Book of Job. To my recollection, I have never heard a sermon or even a lesson about the absolute worst way to console a suffering friend displayed by Job's companions even though it takes up the majority of the Book of Job itself. Not to mention that God is angrier with these men and their counsel than He is with Job for questioning God's goodness. This is evident in Job 42:7 where God says to Eliphaz, "I am angry with you and your two friends, for you have not spoken the truth about me, as my servant Job has."

The scene starts out very pleasantly in verse 11 of Chapter 2 of Job. When Job's three friends heard about the adversity that happened to Job, each of them came from his home, met together to go, and comforted him. So far it all sounds good, right? They even sat on the ground with Job for seven days and nights, and no one spoke. This still sounds like these are some true friends, those that just come to be with their companion at his lowest point.

Then Job cannot stay quiet any longer. He begins to verbally express the utter devastation that has dwelled within him for the past week. Job begins, in Chapter 3, to curse the day he was born for twenty-six verses. Once Job has finished speaking, one of his "friends," Eliphaz, has a response. His response, and the response of the other companions, are the same in each discourse throughout the remainder of the book. These friends all believe, wrongfully, that God is angry and is punishing Job.

For the majority of the Book of Job, these friends accuse him time and time again of committing some sin for which he is receiving the wrath of God. Job defends himself over and over that he has done nothing to be placed into the same category as the wicked.

Doesn't this still hold true today? Don't we immediately rush to the conclusion that when a particular tragedy falls upon a believer, they must have done something sinful? Worse yet, these companions offer no encouraging words to Job at all. They even come down on him that much more when he speaks about losing trust in the goodness of God. And yes, Job does talk about losing his trust that God is good and fair, another immeasurable lesson from the Book of Job that is not fully presented in today's church. However, Job still exhibits remarkable faith in God even though he no longer trusts Him. He agonizes over the lost closeness with God.

Over and over, for the vast majority of the book, there is this exchange between Job and his companions. They begin to accuse and cast blame on Job for something he did either knowingly or unknowingly. Job is even accused of exploiting the poor for his own advantage.

Is this not the same tactic the great accuser himself, Satan, used in the first two chapters? Isn't this the same method he has used on believers since the dawn of time? Telling us that we are unworthy, that we are beyond redemption, that we are in fact unforgivable. And here we see these companions of Job speaking in the same manner of accusatory condemnation all the while believing they represent God and are doing what is best for Job.

If we dig deeper into the responses of these companions, we can see their understanding of God and His ways are very limited. This is just as important and valid today because it speaks to the heart of the typical comment made by unbelievers, which is, "If there is an all-loving God, then why does evil still exist?"

After Job speaks honestly with his friends and insists that he did nothing to be deserving of being treated like a sinner by God, why did they not reevaluate and change their counsel? Why instead did they, even more fervently, continue with their harsh criticism of Job as being untruthful with them and, more so, with himself? Why did Eliphaz accuse Job of committing sins he had made up?

It seems the faith of Job's friends was even more rooted upon the retribution principle. Good things come to those who love God and remain in His will, and destruction comes to the wicked who reject

God and His commands. But it appears for Eliphaz, there is an even bigger concern. In Job 15:4, Eliphaz says, "But you even undermine the fear of God and hinder meditation before him." What is Eliphaz's real concern here? Seems that Eliphaz is concerned that if Job is right, then everyone will stop worshipping, giving to the poor, praying, etc.

Eric Ortlund says it this way: "Eliphaz's worry is that if it gets out that Job really is innocent and is suffering regardless—it is possible to serve God scrupulously for decades and have it, as it were, count for nothing—then no one will serve God at all. The unstated premise here is that people only get into a relationship with God for the blessings that accrue to obedience; otherwise (Eliphaz thinks) we are serving God for no reason."[16]

Ironically, the very thing that Satan predicted that Job would do if God removed His protection from Job is the very thing that Eliphaz believes would happen to everyone who worshipped God if this becomes common knowledge. This becomes clearer as the Book of Job proceeds because the more Job's companions speak, the less they bring God into the conversation. This thought is very uncomfortable for not only Job's friends but everyone throughout the ages. The fact that if this happened to Job, a man in which God said, "No one else on earth like him, a man of perfect integrity, who fears God and turns away from evil." Then it can happen to them, and it terrifies believers.

Which, to me, is precisely the point behind the entire ordeal of Job. To prove not only to Satan but to Job himself, his companions, and the world that we should and can love God purely because He is our Creator. Because He is God.

I have not detailed all the mistakes Job's companions made in their effort to "comfort" their friend; that is not the intent of this book. Eric Ortlund's book, *Suffering Wisely and Well*, does a far greater service to this topic than I could do. But I would like to summarize from his book the lessons on how not to comfort those who are suffering.

---

[16] Eric Ortlund, *Suffering Wisely and Well: The Grief of Job and the Grace of God* (Wheaton, Illinois: Crossway, 2022), 17, 73, 128.

First do not blame the sufferer. They may be blaming themselves far more than you realize for something that may have happened that you have no idea about. Possibly even for something they failed to do rather than something they did.

If our relationship with God was purely based upon the retribution principle alone, do you honestly think that Job would have knowingly committed a sin so grievous that it would cost him almost everything? Would the man with perfect integrity have placed all His children in jeopardy willfully? Would any one of us deliberately put our loved ones, our livelihood, or ourselves at risk if we knew the outcome?

Next, do not speak as if you have been given some special spiritual insight. This is what I would call the pious response. As believers, we always want to rush to be the voice of God when dealing with someone who is suffering. A quick public service announcement here, Jesus is already at the right hand interceding on our behalf. I don't think he needs any help from us in this area. Job's companions believed they were speaking for God and got it completely wrong. As mentioned earlier, they provoked an even harsher response from God than Job did. These friends tortured Job instead of comforting him. They also unwittingly advanced Satan's agenda against Job.

Be careful and always question yourself before speaking to the sufferer. Always ask yourself who it is you are trying to make feel better, them or yourself. There is always a temptation to subconsciously comfort ourselves in the things we say.

Additionally, do not try to fill the comforting role that only God can provide. It is not until God speaks to Job that He is satisfied, reconciled, and most of all, comforted. Similarly, when we are walking with someone who is suffering, we cannot fix them. We are powerless to solve their situation, resolve their trauma, or speak to their protests. We are woefully inadequate to do what only God can for this person.

Resist the temptation to lecture or correct things the person may say. Speaking from experience, I am very dismissive of being lectured by someone, especially the older I get. And to have been lectured by someone who has not tasted the bitterness of intense suffering, I most likely would have alienated that person severely. However, God addressed my protests in a direct but gentle way, as I will speak about in the next chapter.

Finally, look for ways to speak to the person suffering that God does not hate them and that the ordeal will not last forever. I did not feel that God hated me, but I did feel that I had been forsaken. And even now that I say that, it does not quite accurately describe what I was feeling toward God. I knew that for everything there is a purpose for believers, but I could not understand what outcome could justify taking away my precious wife from her family.

Many people want to use the statement "time heals all wounds." I heard this said many times and became quite annoyed with hearing the phrase because I don't agree with it. It is God that heals, not time. The passing of time maybe dulls the pain somewhat. But the passing of time does not heal any wound. From my personal experience, it is God that spoke to me in such a way that I was comforted far more than any person could have offered.

God's Response to Job

Just as He spoke to Job and offered no explanation as to why Job had to endure the suffering, Job was comforted and reconciled to God without any answers to his earlier protests.

God's response to Job was not a defense of His sovereignty over mankind. Rather, He responded specifically to Job's ordeal and Job's objections to His plight. Job 38, 39 demonstrate God's gentle and gracious approach to addressing Job's mistrust of God's character. Which also, in itself, demonstrates that Job was completely wrong about his suspicions of God's nature.

These chapters in Job should impart to us as believers with a large amount of humility in realizing the vast number of things we do not know. Humility is a key ingredient in obtaining wisdom. Once, sin entered this world, and along with it the curse, the paradise that was originally created ended. The main byproduct of evil entering the world is pain and suffering. We are arrogant to believe that we will somehow escape this world without enduring pain and suffering at some point in our life.

God begins Chapter 38 of Job by asking a myriad of questions. In Old Testament wisdom texts, questions are a standard means by which wisdom is passed from sage to student to help him grow, not humiliate him.[17] Questions such as, "Where were you when I established the earth? Who fixed the earth's dimensions, what supports its foundations, and who laid the cornerstone of the earth?" God alone is the only one who understands and is in control of the areas in question. But even so, God was taking the role of a teacher trying to get His pupil to get the answer correct rather than embarrass him for having no clue.

Was all this indicative of some angry, selfish, noncaring tyrant as Job had suggested in his protesting? If, as Job had stated, God was indeed a malevolent being, then I don't think His response would have been so gracious. If Job's fears were indeed true about God, then I would imagine God would have been far harsher in His response to Job. Something along the lines of, "How dare you question my authority, mortal!"

By simply the way in which God responded to His servant actually quashed Job's idea that God attacked him cruelly without any reason. God was saying to Job in a very loving way, "Job, you have accused me of being unjust, cruel, and unreasonable, but do you really know what you are talking about?"

For two solid chapters, God asked question upon question to Job with the purpose of getting Job to recognize and admit the enormous lack of understanding he has about the world and, along with that, have Job understand that he has no proof at all based upon his own ignorance to even suggest that God has been negligent in His role as the sovereign of the universe.

Recall that Job wanted to argue his case, as in a court of law. However, in Chapter 9, Job readily admits that he would not be able to answer God "once in a thousand times," and concludes further in

---

[17] Eric Ortlund, *Suffering Wisely and Well: The Grief of Job and the Grace of God* (Wheaton, Illinois: Crossway, 2022), 17, 73, 128.

Chapter 9, verse 33, that "There is no one to judge between us, to lay his hand on both of us." Meaning that God is the final and ultimate judge of His creation, and there is no other. But in many places throughout Job, he wanted to argue his case before God.

This is a key step in Job's reconciliation and restoration. For us to realize, as Job did, the overwhelming limits we possess in understanding the world and how it operates. But most importantly that God demonstrates each day that He is at the controls of the world. He is the sustainer and provider of His creation. God maintains the greatest care for His creation even in establishing the limits that evil and disorder are allowed to coexist.

Just imagine if God did not keep evil on a tight leash. There is a thought that evil is the leviathan that God is describing in Job 41 instead of an actual beast. When read within this context, this chapter becomes a very different and powerful key piece of information being presented to Job. Essentially God is saying that if it weren't for me, man would have been consumed long ago without any possible way of escaping this beast.

Couple the understanding that we know very little with the fact that everything we have in this life is borrowed. Even the breath we take each day is a gift from God. When we get a firm grasp of these two truths alone, then we can better understand that we are here for His purposes not ours. Then once we understand this, we can be greater witnesses for God in all seasons of life. Both in the good times and the tragic times.

I am not insinuating this will make the pain less or reduce the time it will take to recover from a catastrophe. But it does give us a peace to know that God can take our protests and will respond in the most caring way. He is not a God that tells us to get over it, but He understands and will not turn His back on us even though we may feel abandoned or say and think things, just as Job did, that question God's goodness.

Pain and suffering will distort our vision of the world getting us to focus on all the bad things. However, God will redirect our attention if we allow Him, and remind us that He intended the world to be a wonderful and joyful place. After all, He is the final and ultimate authority.

CHAPTER 5

Answers to My Protests

Just as Job began to protest his circumstances, so did I. Many times I didn't want an answer; many times I demanded one. For every protest that flowed from my mouth or through my mind, God provided me an answer in what was a calm, patient, almost audible question, just as He had questioned Job. I want to share the insight I was given during what was the darkest time in my life. This chapter is the main goal I wanted to accomplish by writing this book. Which is to simply testify to how God, and God alone, pulled me out the ashes and hopefully help someone else who is enduring suffering themselves.

It Is Not Fair

I thought we were doing everything we were supposed to be doing as a Christian couple. I thought we were, happily checking off all the biblical commandments. I, too, thought I had the no-heartbreak insurance policy that all good card-carrying believers feel they have.

But now that I personally was the one who was walking down this dark painful path, I, too, began to declare this was not fair. It was not fair my sons had their mother taken from them at a fairly young age. It was not fair that my youngest, Dallas Aron, would not have his mother there to watch him graduate high school. The one individual who was personally responsible for his entire extraordinary education would not see the end result and bountiful fruit of her labor.

It was not fair that she would not see but one of her sons married and be there beaming with pride as her young men walked down the aisle to adjoin with their spouses. That she would not see Andrew the first to graduate college and get his degree. And I guess the biggest of all was how unfair it seemed that she would not get to enjoy her grandchildren. Something she had dreamed of and was excited to see each one of them come into our lives.

I did not even get past the funeral home visitation when God sent me an answer to my protests of fairness in the form of some old friends who came to pay their respects: Brian and Hannah Julian Brian and his children —Andrew, Caleb, Hannah, and Faith—had endured the exact same event many years prior.

In 2004, while we were still in our hometown in Tennessee, we had a close relationship to a couple, Brian and Rhonda Julian, who were devout Christians as well. Their four children were similar in ages, and they lived just about a mile from us. I went to high school with Rhonda, and her oldest sister was one of my teachers in middle school. Your typical small rural-town relationship where everyone knows everyone.

Our oldest son and their oldest son were the same age and played basketball together at the same middle school. Marla and Rhonda had developed a close friendship and Marla babysat Rhonda's two youngest daughters, Hannah and Faith. All the children were quite young at the time, as the oldest in both our families were around twelve years old. Rhonda was diagnosed that year with a fairly rare form of leukemia. We all were devastated by this news but also hopeful, as Rhonda was otherwise a healthy young lady and was going to begin treatments.

Obviously, we all also were grounded in our faith, and a massive amount of prayer was lifted for her from the entire county and beyond. I remember there being an enormous outpouring of support for this young lady. One of the local businessmen even loaned the family his personal private airplane to fly them out to the West Coast for the treatments.

I had just started running about a year prior and had participated in some 5K road race events. I signed up an organization called Team in Training which primarily raised money for the Leukemia & Lymphoma Society in exchange for training, coaching, and fees to enter an event, such as a half or full marathon. I chose the Music City Marathon in Nashville, Tennessee, and immediately began raising money for Rhonda.

Rhonda fought a hard battle which lasted for quite some time, but she did not beat the cancer and, at a very young age, was taken from this world to her eternal home. I remember thinking on many occasions how unfair it was for this family, especially the children.

God brought them to me and asked me if I thought that I was any better or any more spiritual than Brian and Rhonda. In other words, He asked me, *Do you think you are better than the Julian family?* If one is making a comparison and ranking in terms of severity, then theirs was worse due to the ages of their children. Their youngest daughter, Faith, was a toddler and probably has a very limited memory of her mother.

Just like Job, I was being cross-examined. I was asked, in no uncertain terms, if I felt I had earned a better place than two of the strongest Christians I have known. And I was also reminded that even when events appear to be identical, there can be factors that make one more difficult than another.

A next question I received a little later addressing fairness was this: *Was it fair that Jesus suffered my punishment for my sins?* This is a question that I had heard spoken about before in many ways, although usually within the context of being thankful that we did not have to endure the excruciating pain of the death on a cross. However, I don't believe I recall any discussions surrounding how unfair it was that Jesus endured the torment of being separated from God the Father. This was a different context in which the question was now being conveyed to me.

At this point, I was still bemoaning that it was not fair that I had been separated from my wife. God asked me if it was fair that His Son was separated from Him all because of me. That point hit the mark and stung quite a bit.

You see, you and I are directly responsible for the reason Jesus had to die on the cross and be separated from the Father. But God is not directly responsible for the suffering and pain we endure in this life. Again, our sin is to blame for the effects of this cursed world. Sure, God can intervene in any situation and change the outcome, but He is not the catalyst for the suffering in the first place. Our disobedience caused the separation and curse we have to live with daily.

Why Not Me Instead?

One gift I feel I was given was in the form of a protective nature. I mentioned this very early in this book, but I was a fairly above average boy in stature and physical abilities. I was tall, strong, and fast at an early age. With that, God gave me an inherent nature to protect those who were weaker than me. I remember growing up and rooting for the underdog in almost every situation. For those of you who can remember, one of my favorite Saturday morning cartoons was *Underdog*.

As I grew, this protective nature also amplified, especially with regards to my family. I was ferociously protective of my wife and my sons. So naturally, I shouted at God the question of why it had to be her and not me.

Interestingly, the answer to this question did not come immediately. Also, it was delivered by another source but at God's divine direction.

On one of many occasions, when I was searching for some sort of comfort, I stumbled upon a TEDx Talk by Dr. Mary Neal. Dr. Neal is a board-certified spinal surgeon who drowned on a South American river. Without oxygen for thirty minutes, she was clinically dead. She experienced life after death, conversed with Jesus, and experienced God's all-encompassing love.[18] I owe this lady a debt of gratitude that I will never be able to repay. She is now doing a far

---

[18] Dr. Mary Neal, "Death Brings Context to Life," (2018), https://www.youtube.com/watch?v=C-M9zR17egA&t=432s.

greater work than before in my opinion. I urge you to watch and read her story.

Dr. Neal described what had happened after she drowned. She spoke about being greeted by Christ. And said, "No, I didn't just think or hope it was Jesus. I know it was Christ, just as I would know my husband of thirty years if I had seen him in the grocery store."[19] She goes on to describe being released into heaven and being able to look back at her body being pulled to the shore. She explains that she recognized her body and knew that she was dead.

It was then Dr. Neal went on to say, "But despite having a magnificent life with a wonderful husband and these four young children whom I loved more than life itself, I felt like I was home, and I really had absolutely no intention of returning."[20]

When I heard her say those words, I knew God was talking to me through her. The similarity in that Dr. Neal was close to the same age, had a thirty-year marriage, and had four young children grabbed me as someone grabs another with both hands by the face. The statement she made, without reservation, about feeling at home and had absolutely no intention of returning gave me the answer as to why it was not me. Marla was home, her work here was finished, and she was comforted and was no longer in agony because of the pain from cancer.

Dr. Neal then goes on to describe how she has viewed life since 1999. She details the story of going off to summer camp as a young lady. She described in detail the time she had at the camp as being pleasant and enjoyable. However, the existence of her home and the knowledge that she would be returning to her home brought the context to the time she spent at the summer camp which allowed her to experience it for what it was: a temporary adventure.

As a sidenote, ten years after her experience, Dr. Neal lost her oldest child who was hit by a vehicle. Even after being armed with

---

[19] Dr. Mary Neal, "Death Brings Context to Life," (2018), https://www.youtube.com/watch?v=C-M9zR17egA&t=432s.

[20] Dr. Mary Neal, "Death Brings Context to Life," (2018), https://www.youtube.com/watch?v=C-M9zR17egA&t=432s.

the knowledge of her previous experience, the blissful peace she felt of truly being home, she still asked the question why.

As a follow-up to this response from God via this lady, I was then presented with a secondary question from God addressing my request of, "Why not me?" The follow-up question was, "Would I want Marla to suffer what I was suffering?" The answer to that question was an unequivocal no! Even though I had an unbending need to be the protector of my wife and family, I was instead called to bear the suffering of remaining here. The more I thought about this question, the more I was convinced that I would not want her to be the one who was left behind in this corrupt world.

Mary, my mother-in-law, relayed to me that my dad had once confided in her that he hoped my mother would go before he did. Dad also had this overly protective nature, obviously a nature I inherited. He knew that my mom would not do well without him around. He was absolutely correct.

I saw it happen very quickly after my father was called home. Mom was lost without my Dad. She did not grieve well and did not do well in handling the things that my dad had taken care of in the past. There were times when she would just sit in her living room in silence, staring at the wall. Unfortunately, my mom was obstinate and thought she had the capability to still do things she used to do. But she could not and, at times, was too proud to ask for help. Not only physically but mentally, she had checked out.

Basically, my mom lost the will to live, and within one year and nine months, she left this world also. I don't believe for a moment that Marla would have lost the will to live, but I know she would have been terrified about how she would have been required to provide for herself and our youngest son.

This would have put an enormous burden upon my sons if their mother had been left alone. As this overt need to protect my loved ones was passed to me, my sons also have this wonderful trait. I am very proud of that fact because I believe this is a crucial characteristic of a godly man. One that is missing from the majority of today's males, and we see each day the consequences of those who will not stand up for the weaker in our society. It is enraging when some male feels the need to pick on a weaker person, but what is even more galling are the male bystanders who do nothing. And yes, I use the term male here because that is not a man.

By contemplating both Dr. Neal's testimony and the follow-up question from God, I came to the realization that I was actually still the one who was chosen to continue to guard my family. With that shift in perspective, I felt thankful that I could still fulfill my commitment as a husband and father. Even though I had no say in the matter, I was given the opportunity to protect my wife from the suffering that I would never want her to experience. I could continue to be a role model to my sons and hopefully demonstrate how to suffer wisely and well for God's glory. Although they are wonderful examples of godly grown men, I can still be there to guide them as they continue to travel down the path of life.

Honor to Suffer for Christ

An effect that was once very prevalent in the world, but that has now almost become extinct, is that of the sense of honor. Not the term that is thrown around so often in today's world. You will hear many say, especially when delivering the acceptance of some type of award, "I am honored to be here." Which could mean they are privileged or flattered to be there. No, I am referring to the sense of honor that is derived from the recognition of a higher authority for one's character or integrity. Remember the honor bestowed upon Job by God and the confidence God displayed in Job's character.

As I continued to study God's Word, the counsel that the apostles Paul and James conveyed regarding trials became more than abstract encouragement. I have read these verses, and there have been sermon upon sermon devoted to endurance in the faith. But during this time, they spoke to me in a different way.

The majority of the time, I suspect, most regard these verses as enduring the trials and tests of the enemy. Especially true for the persecuted early Church believers. We read very early in the Book of Acts, the apostles Peter and John were arrested, on more than one occasion, for healing and preaching in the name of Jesus. In Acts

5:40, the Sanhedrin had the apostles flogged and ordered them not to speak the name of Jesus. Verse 41 reads, "Then they went out from the presence of the Sanhedrin, rejoicing that they were counted worthy to be dishonored on behalf of the name." The apostles were delighted to be whipped because of sharing the good news that Jesus was the Messiah.

Unfortunately, I believe many believers today do not recognize the opportunity a significant trial gives us. Most want to think of being counted worthy as having to do with a physical torture for the faith, something that is very foreign to believers in the United States. This country is so far removed from the persecution of Christians that still takes place across the globe; it is amusing to hear the term persecuted being used here.

Regardless, we need to get a firm grasp upon the fact that we are, and have been, in a spiritual war. The enemy bombards us daily with attacks which one does not see. Producing doubt, anxiety, and fear with the end goal of getting believers to blame God and turn their back to the faith. So when suffering comes to those with a false good-things-only faith, they are scattered and defeated because they begin to question God's goodness. They believe God should protect them from any pain.

But just as Jesus took the excruciating pain—the severe mental anguish, the soul-crushing separation from God—that should have been poured out on me, why would I even consider abandoning Him when, in comparison, the smallest of trial comes my way? That sunk into my soul deeply, and just as the apostles rejoiced, I began to feel honored to have been counted worthy to share a small amount of the suffering that my Savior endured for me.

Believers have an opportunity, when suffering comes our way, to do one of two things. We can be a signpost that points to Christ as the only one who brought us hope and comfort in our lowest point. Or we can believe the lies of the enemy raise the white flag of surrender and settle for this miniscule life we are given while here on Earth.

Prayer

As a Christian, I imagine you are thinking this section of the book will be about me testifying to the power of prayer, right? You would be somewhat correct, but I highly doubt it is going to be the way in which you would typically expect.

Right upon the heels of the insight given from the passages speaking about considering it great joy when you face various trials (James 1:2)—which, by the way, the original Greek word used here for trials can also be translated as proving—a still, small whisper from the Holy Spirit reminded me of something I had prayed for several years prior to this ordeal. What I had asked God for, on more than one occasion, was to be more like Christ.

As you might imagine, the feeling of honor to have been considered worthy to suffer like Christ, plus the reminder of what I had asked for earlier, hit me like a sledgehammer to the stomach. Keep in mind, I had just questioned God, through a waterfall of tears, as to why He did not hear our collective prayers for Marla to be healed. It is very difficult to accept that the thing you asked God to give you would be dispensed by the death of the one you love the most.

As you might expect, what I meant when asking to be more like Christ was to be more loving, generous, kind, and compassionate to my fellow man. Not once did it cross my mind to share in the suffering Christ bore on my behalf. But I have come to realize with the passing of time that only God is capable of working out things in such a way as to achieve what we may think is a straightforward answer but in reality is not so easy. I was given more of the traits I mentioned above, but in such a way that I would most likely not have obtained otherwise. Plus, Marla was completely healed from the debilitating disease that ravaged her body, but it meant that she was taken on to her glorious eternal home.

I know that for me, this was a very revealing lesson in accepting the answers that are not exactly presented in the way we had in mind. It is also an extremely difficult lesson to comprehend. Even Christians have become somewhat entitled in their thinking: to believe that there is only one answer or solution to a request, especially in light of the fact that we are presenting our request to the God of the universe. The all-knowing, all-powerful, all-present being who knows the end result of history before it is written. Do we fail to realize—or worse, fail—to believe that He can orchestrate our lives far better than we could comprehend?

There was a period of time, when I was crying out in protest, that I questioned why even pray. If God knows what is the best course of action for believers, why petition for there to be an alteration in the plan? I was reminded that I have absolutely zero control over the events in my life. I became very cynical when listening to prayer requests from people who have not yet walked down the path of having your requests appear to go unheard, especially when the basic all-encompassing request that all believers have voiced at one point in their life was circulated. You know the one: "Please pray." I immediately would think in my mind, *Pray for what?* What outcome are you seeking and are you prepared for the response to not align with the outcome you expect? Are you equipped to handle the answer to the prayer when it is the opposite of what you wanted?

Another aspect of prayer that I began to critique was the vast majority of publicly disseminated prayer requests involve healing from some sort of ailment. Maybe I was being overly critical at the time, but I would question, Why is it we only request prayer when it seems there is no other course of action? Why is the request sent out after someone is admitted to the hospital? Why are we not praying for other possibly more important aspects?

After having lived through my wife battling cancer, a significant question that caused me to really struggle with was, For whose benefit are we asking for healing? Believers throw this verse from Paul so often: "For me, living is Christ and dying is gain" (Philippians 1:21). But I don't get the indication the majority really believe what this verse says because time and time again, the prayer request is for healing for a believer. If we really believe this verse, then is the request of healing really to benefit the one who is sick, or is it to protect the loved ones from pain?

The answer I would give was that it was undeniably for me. I could not bear the thought of living without Marla. I watched her endure severe pain daily as the cancer destroyed her body. I could not stand to see her suffer the way she did, but I also could not let her go! Even when I knew beyond a doubt where she was going. The pain would be no more, and the tears would be wiped from her eyes by the one who suffered for us so that we could be with Him. I was terribly selfish and should have been pleading with God to end her suffering as quickly as possible, which would have basically asked God to either heal her or take her—whichever was His will.

But I was being so short-sighted for someone who has placed their faith in God. One who says he trusts in the promises that God gives us in His Word, but I was an abject failure in actually grabbing and holding onto those promises. And just as God was gentle in His response to Job, so He was with me. Without Christ walking with me, carrying me at times, I could not have made it through this time.

I have always gravitated more to the lessons and commands that came directly from Christ Himself in the Gospels. After the cynicism subsided, I began to think about the model prayer Jesus gave the disciples in Matthew 6. Jesus said in Chapter 6, "When you pray, don't babble like the idolaters, since they imagine they'll be heard for their many words. Don't be like them, because your Father knows the things you need before you ask Him. Therefore, you should pray like this." And then He begins the model prayer which almost every believer has, or should have, memorized.

I find it rather interesting to dissect the passages about prayer from the one who is receiving the appeals. First, we are told not to babble. The Greek word used here is *battalogeo*, which also can be interpreted as "meaningless repetition." Jesus is telling us to not repeat the same things over and over thinking that you will be heard for much speaking. He then tells us that the Father knows the things we need before we ask. If you think about this beyond the daily physical needs of the body, Jesus is saying that God the Father knows what you need in all areas of your life. The mental strength to weather an upcoming storm. The spiritual strength to flee from temptation that is around the corner. And ultimately, the grace we will need when we fail in both arenas because we have placed our faith in ourselves and not in His Word.

Jesus says in verses 9 and 10, "Pray like this. Our Father in Heaven, Holy is Your Name. Please establish and make Your kingdom appear. Your Will be done, or let it be done as You have determined, on Earth as it is in heaven." Not your will be done, if it matches up with my will of what I want to be done. I am limited in what I can understand about any given situation, but God knows the outcome, all outcomes.

To me, this is the crucial part of this model prayer for Christians to really understand. We are asking for things to take place just as God has determined is best. Not as we would have done but as the one who knows the final outcome. The one has determined what is needed to achieve the best end result for us. Do I think there are multiple options? Absolutely. To think otherwise is to limit the all-powerful Creator of the universe. Actually, what I believe that takes place is what Paul is saying in Romans 8:28, "We know that all things work together for the good of those who love God: those who are called according to His purpose."

We make a mess out of things, just as I catalogued earlier with my own life. We make wrong choices and poor decisions. However, for those who love God, He will take this absolute dumpster fire we have created and turn it into a breathtakingly beautiful tapestry. But we must concede and understand that what we ask for may not be answered in the way we want, but that we are completely confident that God is doing what He has determined is best for us. If we don't keep this in the forefront of our minds, we easily fall into the trap of questioning God and His motives.

Jesus goes on to say in verses 11 and 12, "Give us today our daily bread." Or give us our portion of food sufficient for today. "Forgive us our debts as we also have forgiven our debtors." *Trespasses* has also been used here for debts. Another figurative translation is offence or sin. Another way of thinking about this part of the prayer is asking God for forgiveness of our sins as we forgive those who sin against us.

Finally, we are told in verse 13 to ask that the Father not bring us into temptation, which has been a source of debate throughout history, and still is for many today. The question of God the Father leading us into situations that would tempt us to sin. The Greek word here is *peirasmos*, and this word has several meanings associated with it—two of which are a "trial" or "proving." I believe we are being told to request that God keep us from trials to prove our faith. In other words, we are asking that God keep us from adversities that would test our faith.

The next piece of this verse then says, "But deliver us from the evil one." Another word that can be used here instead of *but* is the word *nevertheless*. To understand this difficult verse, another way of thinking about it would be, "…and keep us from trials that would test our faith, nevertheless deliver us from Satan." We are requesting that we be kept from adversities but acknowledge that God is the only one who can deliver us from the Evil One.

I personally have strayed far from this template on how to pray; it is not even similar. I have asked for the things I wanted, for circumstances to proceed as I have determined is best. As with many of the commands of Christ, we fail to adhere to them or believe we need to improve upon them in some way. But here Christ tells us that God the Father knows the things we need before we ask. Does that mean we don't need to make our requests known, or because God has already determined the outcome, we are wasting our time? No, it does not.

We are also instructed, right after the model prayer, in Matthew 7 to keep asking, seeking, and knocking. As I said, I believe there are many options God can use in accomplishing what He knows is best. But what it does tell us is that when we have prayed and pleaded for a course of action that does not happen, we then must understand that God knows something we don't. He has a reason that we don't realize and may never know this side of heaven.

It is much easier said than done. After grasping this message from the Holy Spirit, I did not want to know the reason for the unanswered request for Marla's healing. Recall that Job did not receive a direct answer for why he endured his ordeal. And after receiving the response from God, he apparently no longer felt the need to have an answer. I, too, no longer had a desire to know the reason why.

This is also counter to all the messaging in American culture which inundates you constantly to get what you want and to do what you want in all facets of life. Somewhere along the way, believers have substituted how we were instructed to pray by Jesus Himself to running down our laundry list of our wants and desires. Never once stopping to think, "Is what I am asking going to produce the best outcome?"

We have also been somewhat misled into believing Jesus to be some type of genie in a bottle. When Jesus told the disciples in John 14:13–14, "Whatever you ask in My name, I will do it so that the Father may be glorified in the Son. If you ask Me anything in My name, I will do it."

By praying "in Jesus's name," we believe, on a certain level, we will be guaranteed the answer just as we want it, but we are not told in these verses that is the case. Jesus doesn't say, "Whatever you ask in My name, I will do it just as you wish." No, He says, "So that the Father may be glorified in the Son." We must then realize that the exact opposite of what we are asking may bring greater glory to the Father.

Additionally, these statements from Jesus come after the Last Supper with the disciples, and we are not given any indication whether this statement was or was not specifically for the disciples only. Nevertheless, I have come to realize and believe that these two factors tie right back into how we were taught to pray: by first and foremost to pray that the Father's will be done, and not our will. Still making our requests known to God but remembering that it is for His glory through the Son, and that Jesus may answer these requests in a very different way from what we think is best.

CHAPTER 6

For Widowers

This chapter deals with the primary reason I felt called by God to undertake the writing of this book. This chapter is specifically directed at Christian men who are either dealing with a potential terminal health diagnosis for their wife, or for those who share the same classification that I do of widower. There are significantly less widowers in the United States than widows. According to www.statista.com, in 2021 there were 11.61 million widows to 3.58 million widowers. That's almost a four-to-one ratio. This is most likely part of the reason there are far few resources for men who need help when faced with this dilemma.

Another reason is the traditional way the American society views men. Men should not need help; they are the stronger ones and bear the primary responsibility of managing the family problems. To be strong for our families, men tend to put on a brave front and only grieve periodically and mostly in private. I definitely fit this mold because I was trying to be strong for my sons. To be a rock for them to rely on when all the while I was drowning.

The disparity was quite evident in the media coverage of the September 11, 2001, World Trade Center attacks. As Herb Knoll documents in his book, *The Widowers Journey*, "Consider that almost three thousand people were killed in the September 11, 2001, terrorist attacks on the World Trade Center, and one-fourth of them were women—many with husbands and children. Yet the coverage following the tragedy focused almost exclusively on widows and fatherless children, with little attention given to widowers."[21]

With that said, let's look at the fallacy with this belief that widowers need to just be a man and "get over it." Here are some interesting statistics that Mr. Knoll includes in his book:

- Widowers have a higher suicide risk. According to studies, they are anywhere from almost twice as likely (Social Science Quarterly, December 2009) to three times as likely (Social Science Medicine, 1995) as married men to commit suicide. The risk is even higher for widowers who are either younger or older. Those over age seventy-five are ten times more likely than widows to commit suicide, and widowers under thirty-five are seventeen times more likely to commit suicide than married men (American Journal of Public Health, 2002).
- Widowers are more likely than married men to die in an accident or from alcohol-related causes, lung cancer, or heart disease during the first six months following their loss.
- When men are widowed, they often slip into bad behaviors, such as driving recklessly, drinking, smoking, and eating unhealthily.[22]

I can attest that these are very real problems even for a man who has his faith firmly placed in Jesus Christ. There becomes this dangerous prevailing feeling that you just want to be where your wife is. I say dangerous not because of the thoughts that you want to harm yourself but primarily because you are supplanting Christ with an idol, your wife. We have been commanded to love our wives as Christ loves the church, but we should not love them so much that we unwittingly put them in the place of Jesus. Jesus even addressed

[21] Herb Knoll, *The Widower's Journey: Helping Men Rebuild After Their Loss* (Herb Knoll, 2017), xvii, 54.

[22] Herb Knoll, *The Widower's Journey: Helping Men Rebuild After Their Loss* (Herb Knoll, 2017), xvii, 54.

this himself in Luke 14:26 where He says, "If anyone comes to Me and does not hate his own father and mother, wife and children, brothers and sisters—yes, and even his own life—he cannot be My disciple." A difficult verse to really grasp, but one which essentially says, "Jesus above all else." God and God alone as I said earlier.

What you have known for many years—for me, it was twenty-three years, but for other couples, like my parents, more than fifty years—is suddenly gone. You have been with each other exclusively each and every day. When that ends, you are completely lost, and the dark thoughts invade. If you are a believer, the enemy pounces with the same lies they have been using since time began. And yes, you do start to have the who-cares or what-does-it-matter thoughts enter your mind. This leads to the unfortunate outcomes shown in the bullet points above.

I, too, was in situations, either driving or walking, where I thought to myself, *Go ahead and hit me. I don't care.* I was not being careless, but I was also not at all concerned about my safety in the least bit. When part of a man's, especially a Christian man's, purpose in life has been removed, there is a black hole-sized void that needs to be filled. And just like a black hole, the vacuum produced by this void will pull in whatever it can to try and fill the hollowness.

There were a couple of thoughts I would focus on to aid in overcoming this barrage of attacks from the enemy. First I reminded myself there were four young men who needed their father because they had just lost their mother. How could I take both their parents from them intentionally?

Next, I knew how disappointed Marla would be in me for being a coward and leaving her sons by themselves. Thankfully, I have been involved in athletics and am a very active person. The concept of never giving up has been engrained into my personality both from a physical perspective but also from a spiritual perspective as well. Christ never gave up on us. Since I was an active person, all I wanted to do was work to help cope with the grief. I would stay as busy as I could, either working out or working around my house to make improvements.

Sadly, the disproportion for widows versus widowers is also evident in the church. The church seems to be lacking drastically in ministering to widowers. There was a general grief class that the church I attended offered. It was also deeply evident when I was invited to and attended my first widow/widower luncheon in our church. I was the only man present and, by far, the youngest attendee. Needless to say, I have not been back.

We need to implore our churches to do a better job in equipping our men to handle when the "till death do us part" becomes reality. We need to be there to help our brothers avoid the list of snares which was previously discussed. Simply to say "trust in the Lord" without giving them the means by which to do that is not enough. I know firsthand that churches fail miserably in this area. In my case, once the body had been put into the ground and the memorial service had concluded, the church engagement ceased. Just like Job's companions, people become paralyzed in how to comfort a suffering friend.

In our case, I was the provider, and Marla was the executive of the home. Her passion was to feed and nurture her family. Consequently, neither I nor my sons had any skill at all in preparing meals. An additional piece of advice would be to begin now to learn how to prepare food and to teach your children to do the same. It also will give your spouse some needed rest from the daily duty of meal preparation. I believe it will be a welcome surprise for them. A regret that I have is that I did not spend more time with her in the kitchen simply helping her, as best I could, in doing the thing she loved.

Advice for Those Who Want to Help

I remarked a little in Chapter 3 about how uncomfortable people on the outside are with someone who is in the midst of profound grief. They desperately want to help but are at a loss for what to do or what to say. I saw this manifest itself in many different ways with some of my closest friends during the memorial services and the months afterward. Remember, this is coming from a male perspective and is designed for widowers, not so much widows.

As I have said earlier, men and women grieve differently, but society seems to think that men don't need help. I am here to tell you that yes, we do. The evidence is in the statistics above with a large portion of men careening out of control just trying to deaden the pain.

I have maintained, to a certain extent, some very long-term dear friends. These are people I went to school with for many years, in some instances more than ten. But during this time, they were at a loss for how they could be there for me. They didn't express this verbally to me, but I could see it in their struggle to figure out what to say. I recognized they were trying to be as delicate as they could, which was appreciated, but at the same time it almost felt patronizing. I was, after all, a grown man, not a child.

There were some who had a better grasp on how to help, two specifically who happened to be very old and very dear friends, Connie Gunzel and Angie Dickenson. I have known these two special friends since very early in elementary school and count them as my sisters. They were just there for me even though it had been years since we had spoken to each other. Without these two special friends, it would have been exponentially harder to have gotten through the months which preceded Marla's death. But most of my friends were struggling with how they could be of consolation. This is quite all right; I never expected anyone to be able to alleviate the pain. This would have been extremely disappointing and enormously unfair to place that kind of expectation upon any person.

First I want to stress again that everyone is different in how they are going to handle grief. Especially the suffering that is to follow with the separation of the one you love the most. However, I would like to give some suggestions from what I experienced personally and what I have gathered in researching about grieving.

Don't feel like you have to say something comforting or profound. The term I hated to hear the most was, "Sorry for your loss." I wanted to shout back at everyone who said this, "I haven't lost anything. I know where she is!" I personally became very aware of my words when I interact with someone who is grieving. I have made it a priority to say, "You have my deepest condolences."

I know this may sound a little too formal when dealing with someone who is close to you, but for me it was far more encouraging than "sorry for your loss." But you can communicate far more non-verbally than you might realize. Just to have someone look at me with sympathy in their eyes while they were giving me a hug spoke more to me than anything they could have said. Don't search for words to say; simply find a way to show you understand, that you care, and that you will be there for the person.

Which leads me to the next recommendation. Don't be afraid to talk about the loved one who has just passed. All people are different, so this will vary; but for me, to hear someone recall a past experience with my wife gave me a reprieve from the thoughts of having to live without her. I remember it seemed to be the same with the individuals who were in the grief sharing class I attended. It seemed that each person in the class wanted to talk about their loved one and were delighted when others were interested in hearing more about the person. Some were much more forthcoming; others were more reserved, but it seemed to bring a change in demeanor when each individual was given the opportunity to share memories about their loved one.

This next suggestion is one that is probably the hardest. I am as guilty as anyone on this one, and I obviously have been on the receiving end; but unfortunately, I have failed on the giving end also. Make a conscious effort to be there for the person after the memorial service has ended. I know for everyone daily life gets in the way. Each individual goes back to their day-in, day-out routine and concentrate on the things in their own life. One of the hardest things for me was the solitude once the services had ended.

There were a few close friends who made it a priority to stay connected with me afterwards. The sisters I spoke of earlier and a dear lady from the homeschool group who had lost a newborn knew the difficulties of grieving. But as you may have noticed, these were women who are far more emotionally aware than men. Men need to get involved with their friends who may be grieving. Make it a priority to take them out and engage in some type of activity even if it is just dinner.

Even if it's just taking the person for a walk, and let them—if they want—express the emotions they are feeling. Allow them to just get it out, whatever emotion it may be. Do not feel as if you are required to offer any sort of wisdom even if you have walked this path before. Don't be surprised if there are some questions or protesting that takes place that you may feel is uncharacteristic of this person's beliefs. Above all, resist the urge to "correct" your friend in what they may say. I am sure God expects the questions to come; however, His amazing grace never wavers.

Offer to continue to provide meals, especially if the loved one that passed was the meal preparer. For me, this was a huge new problem to tackle. Marla was very fulfilled in her role as mother and homemaker. She would hardy ever relinquish her duties to cook for her family even when she was sick. As such, this was a huge obstacle to overcome.

Our small church group had provided many, many meals during her illness, of which I am extremely thankful. But almost as soon as the memorial services ended, the support ended. It's as if people think, *Well, they have been buried, so it's over.* But in reality, the suffering is only starting. Even one or two meals a week would have been so helpful as we began the process of adapting to the change. This is especially critical for a widower who may have become a single parent.

Moving Forward

Finally, I would like to leave you with a word about moving forward with your life. The absolute hardest, most gut-wrenching painful thing I endured (and there were many) was hearing my wife tell me that I would find love again as she lay dying of cancer. I remember Marla telling me that Rhonda Julian had also confided in her, during the last days of Rhonda's life, that she had met the woman who would raise her children. Marla had also confided in Misty, her sister, that I would not have a problem finding someone because I was so good-looking.

The moment Marla told me and said these words, I became physically ill. Not to mention I was already in excruciating mental anguish, and this was the absolute last thing I wanted to hear from my beloved. At some point later on, I realized that you don't think about the things that would cause jealousy in a relationship during this type of ordeal. Rather, you just want to be assured that your loved one who remains will be cared for and not left alone. Wanting them to be cared for, protected, and given the caring support just as she had done for twenty-three years.

As I said in the beginning of the book, don't rush to fix what you as a man perceive as broken. Another piece of advice I did receive during the early stages of grief was not to make any significant decisions within the first year of any traumatic event. Although everyone processes things differently, do not let anyone tell you what grief timeline you should follow. That is solely your decision; however, I believe this advice has a great deal of merit.

I became curious sometime around November of 2018. Recall that Marla had just went home to Jesus in September of 2018. I had zero idea of what to do, so seeing all the advertisements, I visited an internet dating site. If you are unaware, to even browse, you are required to open an account; so I did. I recognized very quickly that it was way too early for me. I was nowhere near ready and was overcome with unbelievable feelings of guilt after simply passing a few messages with a couple of women. I quickly closed the account and did not even think about it until around the fall of 2019 after my mother passed.

A big factor in rethinking the idea of dating came from my sons. As I was talking with Jacob one day, the issue came into the conversation. Jacob told me that he did not want to see me become a bitter old man. He didn't say as much, but I believe I was traveling the path to become just that. I can attest that I had become very cynical. My other sons agreed with the idea that I needed to seek out some companionship.

To hear this come from your children helps tremendously in dealing with the feelings of guilt. As the one that remains behind, for me anyway, there is this overwhelming sentiment that you need to continue to suffer in honor of your spouse. I believe it goes along with the response to the protective nature that you wish it were you instead.

So somewhat reluctantly, I reopened the dating app account and ever so slowly began to stick my toe in the water. This is an enormously discouraging process for trying to find what you have no idea in the first place what you are looking for. Nevertheless, I primarily messaged ladies but met very few in person and had one actual date.

The biggest thing I learned during this time was that most ladies look at a widower as if they are broken. Which I find very befuddling because a widower fulfilled their vows, whereas a divorced man negated his vows to God and the woman he married. So I am somehow worse than a divorced man? I remember one lady that I actually met for coffee, telling me, "Oh, that's not been that long ago," in reference to the death of my wife.

After several months, this was the most frustrating thing I have tried to do. Many would not even respond, many only wanted to message, and those who seemed to be interested in actually meeting were a several-hours drive away. The women who were the closest in my own area were the worst. I gave up and closed the account again; it was useless.

In late 2019, I did have one woman contact me, which did progress past one meeting; but to my exasperation, there were early indications that I would be asked to forget my past. Statements were made that some things I had, like pictures of my wife, would make this woman uncomfortable. I was not about to box up my past life and put it into storage as if it never happened. I could not or would not do that. Finally, after having moved to a different dating app, which produced the same results, I had given up. But here is where God intervened as only He can.

I am not one for wasted efforts and had had enough of these pointless games that take place on dating apps. I came across this beautiful lady whose profile name was "TX Girl" in South Carolina. I reviewed her profile and noticed she had three children who were the same ages as three of my boys. I thought that was very positive. But I distinctly remembering thinking that this lady will probably not respond to my messages because that had been the norm, so I was not going to even try.

Looking through her pictures, she had included one from a Spartan race she had participated in. I had participated in a Spartan race in November of 2018. I simply asked her, "How did you like the Spartan race?" This was the last attempt. I did not believe she was going to respond, so I stopped looking and was done trying completely.

However, God had other plans. He brought another very special lady into my life. One picture; if she had not included that one picture from the Spartan race, I would not have sent her a message. The odds that she would include this one picture from her Spartan race were, in my estimation, extremely small. She responded, we met, and I was very at ease and had this feeling as if I had known her for a long time. I felt God's hand in it from the start. Two years later, we are engaged to be married.

For you who may be struggling, as I did at first, regarding dating and the idea of remarrying, here is one of the most insightful pieces of advice from Carole Brody Fleet: "When it comes to love, our hearts are truly without capacity or limits—if this were not the case, we would each have only one child because how could our hearts possibly expand to love more than one? We all have an infinite capacity to love, and should that be a widowed's choice, finding love in a new life can and should absolutely be part of their dynamic. Love is also not mutually exclusive one of the other. Loving again does not mean that the love for a late beloved somehow goes away. It doesn't. Furthermore, loving again does not dishonor or disrespect the person who is no longer here, nor does it disrespect the memory of that person. This is a concept that can create a fair amount of discord (especially within families) when a widowed finds companionship or love once again."[23]

This was not written from a Christian perspective, but I wholeheartedly believe that God gave us an unlimited capacity to love. We

23 Carole Brody Fleet, *Forget-Me-Never: The Reality of Remarriage After Widowhood* (www.huffpost.com/entry/remarriage-after-widowhood, 2013).

are created in His image, and He is infinite love. The simple fact that He has not obliterated the vile human race is proof itself.

I also feel that this is a way to honor the lessons I learned from Marla about how to love better—to take those lessons and improve upon them even more. Not only did she have an unbelievable impact upon my dad on how to exhibit his love but she taught me so much about how to love more completely. Ms. Fleet concludes by saying, "Remarriage does not equal forgetting—let no one tell you otherwise. Loving again does not imply lack of or the end of love for the past. You are not destined to remain in mourning forever…that isn't why you are here. Embrace and carry forward the legacies that were entrusted to you by your late beloved. If you choose it, living your new life can include companionship…and love. Choose carefully, choose wisely—and love again abundantly. Because you can."[24]

Thinking about it in the context of God's sovereignty, I am humbled that He allowed me to have one amazingly beautiful lady as my wife and mother of my sons. But for Him to do it a second time with Christina is far more than I ever deserve. To be blessed with another amazingly beautiful woman is beyond my ability to express my gratitude.

God blessed the second part of Job's life more than the first. I am nowhere near the godly man Job was, but for God to bless me with what He has is far more than I deserve. I am not worthy to be given the opportunity to bring glory to Christ in suffering a miniscule amount of the pain Jesus took for me.

As a Christian, we have been given the Comforter to get us through this life. If you are suffering with grief and feel like you have been abandoned or your faith has been tested, God can handle your protests and will speak to you in ways you might not expect.

---

[24] Carole Brody Fleet, *Forget-Me-Never: The Reality of Remarriage After Widowhood* (www.huffpost.com/entry/remarriage-after-widowhood, 2013).

ABOUT THE AUTHOR

Dallas M. Gardner earned a doctorate in pastoral theology in 2008. In 2018, he quickly realized he was mentally and spiritually unequipped for suffering and grief after the passing of his wife, Marla; his father; and his mother within a three-year period.

As a believer in God, are you prepared for suffering and grief that will come your way? After the death of my beloved wife in 2018, I started searching for resources to provide some guidance on how to cope with the intense grief that comes with being a widower at a fairly young age. To my surprise, I found very few publications directed at helping widowers deal with the suffering of losing their spouse and almost nothing from a Christian perspective on the topic.

In the months following my wife's passing, I absorbed as much information on grieving and suffering as I could find. I read about grief and attended grief-sharing sessions at my local church. But I kept questioning why these things happened to my family and why prayers were not heard. I realized that the church as a whole does not do a very good job in preparing the flock for grief and suffering which inevitably will come our way at some point in our lives.

During this period of confusion, doubt, and crying out for answers, God responded to my protests and ultimately provided comfort as only He can. *Why Me, Lord!? Suffering Widower* was written to offer witness to God's unwavering grace and to look into the insights regarding suffering from the Bible, primarily the Book of Job.

Printed in the USA
CPSIA information can be obtained
at www.ICGtesting.com
LVHW050020161023
761014LV00054B/748

9 798887 513812